UNLEASHING
The WORD

In most church services the reading of the Word is poorly and hurriedly done. What a missed opportunity! The public reading of God's Word is an interpretive act that takes skill and thought and has historically been understood as a means of grace equal with preaching and the sacraments. In the books of Ezra and Nehemiah it was the public reading of Scripture that transformed the nation. Max's book will help your church restore this neglected worship practice. There's nothing else like it.

— *Tim Keller*
Pastor, Redeemer Presbyterian Church, New York City
Author, The Reason for God *and* The Prodigal God

I've been personally stirred at conferences where Max McLean made Scripture come alive, and now I'm delighted that this book will inspire and train others to do likewise. Whether people apply these ideas in worship, small group, or family settings, they will lead to more powerful Bible reading, which is an undeveloped way of seeing God's power at work.

— *Tony Evans*
Senior Pastor, Oak Cliff Bible Fellowship
President, The Urban Alternative

In every pivotal moment of my life, the Word of God has been the primary way God has spoken to me. McLean and Bird remind us to let the spoken Word come alive in our communities. For a culture that is tired of words, nothing matches the beauty of God's Word revealed through the voices of the beloved.

— *Dave Gibbons*
Pastor, NewSong Church, Irvine, California
Author, The Monkey and the Fish: Liquid Leadership for a Third Culture Church

I am thrilled to see this book make its way into the hands of church leaders and artists, elevating the power of Scripture in our Sunday morning gatherings. The authors of *Unleashing the Word* communicate their passion for the public reading of the Bible and offer practical strategies that can make a tremendous contribution to the worship experience of many congregations!

— *Nancy Beach*
Champion for the Arts, Willow Creek Association

This splendid book reads just like Max speaking—warm and engaging—and it's filled with practical suggestions for an art that the church needs to reinvigorate.

—*Quentin Schultze*
Arthur H. DeKruyter Chair in Faith & Communication, Calvin College
Author, An Essential Guide to Public Speaking

The Word of God is intrinsically powerful and sharp. If it has become anemic and dull to you or to your audience, Max can help. With practical suggestions he'll help you open up the valve and allow a greater flow of God's Spirit in your reading of the Bible. The Scripture will never sound the same to you—or your hearers.

—*Dave Browning*
Pastor, Christ the King Community Church, Burlington, Washington
Author, Deliberate Simplicity: How the Church Does More by Doing Less

I'm jumping up and down about this book! Finally, there's help with the most neglected three minutes of worship: the Scripture reading. And talk about help. This book shares tips from the performance world about finding the rhythm of the text, authenticity, breathing, voice projection, microphone use, involving kids ... and more. *Unleashing the Word* is the "bible" on reading the Bible out loud!

—*Sally Morgenthaler*
Author, Worship Evangelism *and* The Emergent Manifesto of Hope

What would happen if the contemporary and traditional church took Max McLean's book to heart? I believe we could see a revival that would awaken both seekers and believers to the magnificent power of God's Word. *Unleashing the Word* is a must read for pastors, worship leaders, and laypeople who desire to see lives changed by the creative and passionate reading of Scripture. Max and Warren not only give a rich theological basis for the public reading of the Bible, but also provide practical steps on how to make it happen in your community.

—*Ben Young*
Pastor of Worship Second Baptist Church Houston, Texas
Coauthor of Devotions For Dating Couples

UNLEASHING
*The*WORD

Rediscovering the Public Reading of Scripture

Max McLean
and Warren Bird

ZONDERVAN

ZONDERVAN.com/
AUTHORTRACKER
follow your favorite authors

We want to hear from you. Please send your comments about this book to us in care of zreview@zondervan.com. Thank you.

ZONDERVAN

Unleashing the Word
Copyright © 2009 by Max McLean and Warren Bird

This title is also available as a Zondervan ebook. Visit www.zondervan.com/ebooks.

This title is also available in a Zondervan audio edition. Visit www.zondervan.fm.

Requests for information should be addressed to:

Zondervan, *Grand Rapids, Michigan 49530*

Library of Congress Cataloging-in-Publication Data

McLean, Max.
    Unleashing the word : rediscovering the public reading of Scripture / Max McLean and Warren Bird.
        p. cm.
    Includes bibliographical references and index.
    ISBN 978-0-310-29270-8 (softcover)
    1. Bible — Reading. 2. Oral reading. 3. Reading in public worship. I. Bird, Warren. II. Title.
BS617.M36 2009
264'.34 — dc22   2009018569

Cover design by Ben Geist
Interior design by Matthew Van Zomeren
Printed in the United States of America

---

09 10 11 12 13 14 15 • 22 21 20 19 18 17 16 15 14 13 12 11 10 9 8 7 6 5 4 3 2 1

CONTENTS

CONTENTS
OF THE DVD

1. Readings That Unleash the Word
   Max watches various readers and offers commentary on each one

2. Finding the Right People
   Max discusses how to develop a Scripture reading team

3. Preparing to Read Scripture
   Max explains and demonstrates how he prepares for a Scripture reading

4. Scripture Readings by Max McLean
   Scripture readings of various selected passages by Max McLean

5. Dramatic Presentations of Mark by Max McLean
   Selected dramatic presentations of the Gospel of Mark by Max McLean

6. Credits

FOREWORD

I AM ABSOLUTELY CONVINCED that the books we read mold our lives more purposefully and eternally than we ever realize. The apostle Paul wrote to Timothy from prison, "Bring . . . my scrolls" (2 Timothy 4:13), for a book could set the mind free, breaking the shackles of temporal powers. To that I add, God himself must believe in books or he would not have given us one.

Of course, before we had God's written Word, we had his spoken Word. God spoke the world itself into existence and revealed himself through words. For thousands of years, humankind lived with an oral tradition: every idea, every principle, everything that was considered significant and worthy of pursuit was transferred from generation to generation and kept as a sacred trust by an oral commitment.

Growing up in India I shared this same value. There's a tremendous reverence for words uttered out of the past. "What did your father say about it?" I heard that so often. Ideas were passed on by word of mouth, parent to child, from one generation to the next.

Soon after I left India, I felt the call of God upon my life and entered Tyndale College in Toronto, where I received my undergraduate degree in theology. I will never forget laying my hands on the book *Why Revival Tarries* by Leonard Ravenhill. Oh, the power of that book! I still remember sitting in the library reading it. I was twenty-two years old. I could hardly wait for my lunchtime or the break between lectures so I could get back to this book. From page after page, I made notes and wrote down passages that are with me to this very day.

Some time later, somebody loaned me Ravenhill's recorded sermons on prayer and revival. I listened to them at home hour after hour. I can still hear my mother asking, "Aren't you tired of that man's voice? It's echoing through these walls." Yes, I can still hear his words of such deep penetration into my soul — and the Word of God began to take root in my heart in a way it had not before.

Time and again I have witnessed the awesome power of God's spoken Word. You may hear familiar passages as if you were hearing them for the first time. When his words are received, they bring understanding, repentance, and hope in time of need.

This was my experience when I first heard Max McLean read the Scriptures. His stirring voice and incredible memory are truly gifts from

God. His passionate reading of the Scriptures will make a mark on your life. I have known Max for years. What always amazes me is his ever-present enthusiasm and how deeply he feels what he reads. I listen to him often, during the many hours I spend on the road.

Warren Bird I came to know through his writings during the days I taught in Nyack, New York. He always wanted to write in such a way as to have maximum impact. This team of Max and Warren is a combination that was waiting to happen.

Every reader will be blessed, and I pray that the enthusiasm these two convey will spread as a contagion of health for the soul, to every reader and listener who yearns to hear from God.

—Ravi Zacharias,
author and speaker, www.rzim.com

Why We Wrote This Book

I (WARREN) WAS SITTING IN THE BARBER SHOP. It's often quite a wait, so I had brought a book that I was busy underlining.

"What kind of work do you do?" asked the twenty-something man sitting next to me. Maybe he thought I was working.

When people ask what I do, I can choose between several options, depending on how much conversation I want to invite. If I say "seminary professor" or "minister," it's usually a conversation stopper. If I say "staff at a private foundation," it sounds so safe that they usually offer their own line of work as a more interesting point of conversation. If I say, "I write books," we usually have a lively discussion. I went for the third option.

"What kind of books?" he asked.

"Very good ones," I replied with a smile. Then I clarified, "I write to church leaders."

"Well, I'm a volunteer leader with my church youth group," he offered. "What book are you currently writing?"

"It shows how to make the Bible come alive when someone reads it aloud, such as at church," I explained, referring to this book. "When a congregation gathers for worship, various spiritually minded people bring skill, training, and rehearsal to the music and teaching portions; why not do the same to the Scripture reading as well?"

> When a congregation gathers for worship, various spiritually minded people bring skill, training, and rehearsal to the music and teaching portions; why not do the same to the Scripture reading as well?

"That's really interesting," he said. "*I never thought about it.*"

That reaction represents a major motivator behind this book. It's one we've heard a lot. In fact, at one time it was my own reaction.

My "aha" moment came because I met Max McLean (pronounced muh-CLANE). His approach to the Bible exposed me to a model I'd never seen or heard about—or even thought about. He unleashed God's Word for me in a way I had never experienced before. Convinced that he had found something that could benefit tens of thousands of churches, I bugged him for years to write a book. He finally agreed—if we'd work on it together.

Max takes his own reading of the Bible far beyond what most of us will ever dream of doing. He has memorized entire sections of the Bible—the entire Gospel according to Mark (678 verses), as well as big chunks of Genesis, Acts, all of Philippians, and the Sermon on the Mount.

In addition to his impressive level of personal memorization, Max has produced a daily radio program, *Listen to the Bible*,[1] which is simply him reading the Bible in an engaging way. He's found an appreciative audience for the Scriptures on more than seven hundred radio stations spanning five continents.

Max's reading style—whether fully memorized or just well rehearsed—opened up a whole new world for me, inviting me to engage the Word in ways I had never done before. When he read the Gospels, I felt as if I was right there, hearing them read for the first time. I felt the emotion and pulse of each situation as it unfolded. When Max read from Genesis, the characters came alive. I began to experience some of the drama that Abraham did when God asked him to sacrifice his son, and at the last minute, screamed out, "Do not lay a hand on the boy ... Do not do anything to him" (Genesis 22:12). Wow!

Max has a gift for drawing out the nuances of the text, allowing the Bible to speak in ways that communicate the power and passion of the Word. Listening to Max read has helped me grow closer to God, and I have also gained a better understanding and appreciation for the Bible. I long for others to have that same experience, and I hope that is what will happen as this book unfolds.

STRUCTURE OF THE BOOK AND DVD

Working with Warren, I (Max) have structured the book into four sections. The first four chapters cover my story—why I'm so passionate about hearing God's Word read well, how I got involved in reading on my own and with a team at my church, and what I've seen happen in churches that elevate their Scripture readings. The next section provides specific guidance on how to prepare for a great reading. It also contains fifteen helpful illustrations. The third section describes the many ways you can be a "voice" that raises the quality bar in various settings in which the Bible is read. The final section offers some practical advice on where to go next—what to do after you finishing reading this book, plus a Q&A section. The five appendixes cover things you might say before or after reading, how I prepare a Scripture reading, suggested texts for you to practice, resources I've created through the Fellowship for the Performing Arts, and discussion questions for the DVD.

We've included an instructional DVD with the book as a further aid in developing a ministry of Scripture reading at your church. Scripture reading is more easily caught than taught, so we want to demonstrate some of the main ideas from the book and give you some examples of how volunteers in your church can read the Bible in emotionally engaging, powerful ways.

You can start with either the book or the DVD. The material has only slight overlap; for the most part, the DVD contains material not found in the book. Either resource can be used in a classroom or small group setting.

We're Writing for You

We wrote this book for anyone who wants to learn how to read Scripture in a public setting. The primary context, we assume, will be in congregational worship, but we're aware that in many homes the Bible is read aloud each day as part of family worship or bedtime reading, and Bible reading also occurs everywhere from weddings to hospital visitation. The passion, perspective, and practical insights of this book will certainly apply to each of those contexts. We've also tried to write in a way that allows the book to be useful to those in a wide variety of Christian traditions.

In their book *Getting the Word Across,* Robert Jacks and Gordon Fee begin with a recognition of their own inadequacy, alluding to 2 Corinthians 12:9: "The grace of God is sufficient for everything we do," but we certainly aren't good enough to do it! "You're inadequate because the Lord God made you that way ... There is a God and you're not it.... You're not up to snuff and you've got to depend on God," they affirm.[2] We can't do what God asks us to do, whether it's reading Scripture in church or writing a book, but our inadequacy leads us to greater dependence on the Lord.

All of us suffer from this inadequacy, whether you are a veteran reader, a new reader, or a future reader. We all need help in reading the Word of God—and we all have ways that we can improve. We believe that's exactly the way God wants it to be. As another writer has said so well, "We serve by the endowment of God, at the activation of the Spirit, and for the good of the church."[3] When our hearts and our skills are both aligned toward that end, God does some amazing things!

As the bibliography for this book illustrates, there are a handful of excellent resources already available on how to read the Scripture aloud. We hope that this book serves as a complement to them, not a replacement. That said, we believe this book has several unique features and perspectives. While other books tend to focus on interpreting the various literary styles of the Bible, that is not the focus of this book. Others tend to get into some of the technical elements on the mechanics of good reading, but this book is more story-based, with visual illustrations, focusing on just a handful of techniques—the ones we believe are the most essential—for effective oral reading.

EXPERIENCING THE SACRED VOICE

Warren and I want to help you learn to present the Bible in such a way that your audience can engage the Word with their heart, mind, and soul as they hear it being read aloud. The goal is ultimately transformation—that lives will be touched and changed, just as the original hearers were.

The Bible has long been one of the world's *least-read* bestsellers. According to Zondervan, 91 percent of Americans own at least one Bible, but only 22 percent have read through the entire text. Certainly, the goal of Bible reading is not simply to learn Bible trivia and fill our heads with information. Rather, we want to experience God's transformation, but that won't happen until people experience the Word with all its power. That's the aim of this book: to spread a vision for reading the Scriptures that unleashes the power of God's Word into needy human hearts.

PART ONE

MY STORY

Chapter One

How I Got Started Reading Scripture Aloud

During my childhood, I was quite interested in the idea of God—and a little frightened as well. I grew up in a nominal church-going home, but when I was about fourteen, I made a clean break from anything to do with Christianity. During my college years, I even dabbled a bit in Eastern mysticism.

After college, I was attracted to a Christian woman named Sharon, and we began dating. I didn't really understand her faith, but since I was interested in spending time with her, I would accompany her to church from time to time. She introduced me to some of her friends who were studying the Bible together.

Though I wouldn't normally have any interest in studying the Bible, for some reason, I felt compelled to attend one of their sessions. They had a guest teacher that evening, and I distinctly remember that the teaching failed to engage me. But I found that I was drawn to the Bible passage being read. It was from Galatians 1. The word *Galatians* meant nothing to me at the time, but I remember the words of those verses hitting me in a passionate and forceful way. Prior to that night, I had never been confronted by the power and insight of the Bible. Something was changing.

From that moment, I began to see God working in my life, bringing what I would later come to understand as a conviction of my sins. At first I just wanted to run away, but where can you run to get away from

God? I began reading the Bible for myself, something my nominal faith tradition had never emphasized, and I ended up reading John's gospel in one sitting.

As I read the gospel, it was almost as if I could see, feel, and experience it in my mind's eye. I felt like an eyewitness as Jesus was stepping out of the pages of my Bible. By the time I got to the passion narratives and the crucifixion, I was in tears. When I read about the resurrection, I felt an inexplicable joy overwhelming my entire body.

> Prior to that night, I had never been confronted by the power and insight of the Bible.

At that moment, I knew two things. The story of Jesus was true, and my life would never be the same again.

Today, I recognize that time as a work of God's Holy Spirit, illuminating the words of the Bible, making them come alive, and changing me from the inside out. Since that time, I've seen it happen time after time in the lives of countless people. The words of Scripture are powerful and life-changing, breaking through to the hearts of those who are ready to receive it.

Drawn to Theater

Shortly before meeting Sharon, I had developed a desire to act. I had always had a social phobia when it came to being in front of people, a carryover from my childhood. So during college, I had started acting as a way of overcoming that fear, and it had grown into a love for the stage.

I was born in Panama City, Panama, and I first came to America at the age of four, arriving at the Statue of Liberty in New York harbor. My dad served in the military, so we moved quite a bit growing up, living in places all across the continental United States, the Far East, and Europe.

I think I was attracted to the theater because I had a strong desire to express myself, and acting was able to draw that out of me. I enjoyed connecting to my inner emotions and then expressing those emotions in a controlled way in front of others. As an actor, I knew I was still pretty raw and that I would need a lot of work in the various acting disciplines. That included vocal training. My voice was stuck in a limited range, and it was affecting my ability to accurately express my thoughts and feelings. I planned to do some postgraduate work after college at a drama school in London to develop those skills.

My spiritual birth the year after I graduated from college did not derail those plans at all. In fact, after that experience, I was even more energized than before. I was certain that God would use my training in the dramatic arts, even though I wasn't at all sure how. In 1978, I completed my postgraduate degree in theater and then did some work on the stage in Great Britain, in New York City, and in regional theater.

During this time, Sharon and I got married and started our family (we now have two lovely daughters). Before long, I began to realize that my life as an actor was little more than serving as a hired hand. My job was basically to communicate, as brilliantly as possible, the ideas of other people, regardless of their message. I found it both demanding and unfulfilling.

While I was struggling through this dissatisfaction with my work, God was calling me to experience more of him. He was teaching me that "no one can serve two masters" (Matthew 6:24). Eventually, I felt compelled to leave the theater and abandon acting altogether. (This was my personal pathway, but this book will not argue that people need to leave their primary work or be trained in theater in order to read the Bible effectively.)

FIRST READING
IN CHURCH

Looking back, I know that my departure from the theater at that time was from the Lord, but it still left a huge void in my life. I didn't know what I would do. To fill that void, I became much more active in my local church in Chatham, New Jersey, which was part of the Christian and Missionary Alliance denomination. My pastor, Paul Bubna, preached the Bible with great conviction. He also invited outstanding guest speakers to preach on a regular basis. Over time, I was exposed to great preaching and Bible teaching. I began to enjoy listening to audio tapes of other preachers on my commute to work. I found myself being moved by the insight from their sermons and the conviction in their voices. The way they connected with the Bible and were able to inspire and exhort others intrigued me. Their personal devotion to the Word of God enabled them to communicate with such power that I found it riveting.

I remember my first one-on-one meeting with Pastor Bubna. It was in the spring of 1980. I was still a fairly new Christian. We had breakfast together, and he asked if I would read the Scripture for the following Sunday during the service. It was 2 Peter 3:10–15.

I wanted to do it well, so I rehearsed it carefully. The process of meditating on the Scripture as I prepared to present it really opened me up to receive what God was saying. The text began to warm my heart. That morning, I was asked to sit at the front of the church with the pastor. What an honor that was! I was nervous but also very excited. As I did the reading, I noticed that the congregation listened with unusual attention.

The feedback after the service was immediate and widespread. Their eyes and the gratitude they expressed were a great encouragement to me. So many people I had never met thanked me profusely for allowing them to receive the Scripture in a new light. It was a life-changing day. Little did I know at the time that the Lord had taken away my theater career so that he could use me in an entirely new way.

> So many people I had never met thanked me profusely for allowing them to receive the Scripture in a new light.

In part, the response from the congregation came because my reading was such a stark contrast to what they were used to hearing. Most weeks, the pastor would have the elders pray with him before the service, and then he would ask one of them to read the passage that morning. None of them really had time to reflect on the passage, much less to practice it. These were mature Christians, but few of them had any gift for reading the Scripture aloud to the congregation.

During this time, the Lord gave me another experience that had a profound effect on my life. The church had invited an evangelist to speak at a men's missionary breakfast at 7:30 on Saturday morning. When my alarm clock went off at 6:30 that morning, I almost turned it off, thinking "I'm not going." But for some reason, the Spirit just wouldn't let me off the hook. So I went, dutifully, but without much expectation.

I was in for a big surprise. The speaker was a young evangelist whom I had not heard of. When he started to speak, all my senses lit up. Never before had I heard such dynamic passion and sheer logic combined into a single address. The man's name was Ravi Zacharias (who wrote the foreword to this book). His talk was the most intense, fast-paced, alarming, and at times humorously engaging speech I'd ever heard. I know I didn't fully understand what he was saying, but I did sense that I was in the presence of someone who spoke for God at a deep, profound level.

Ravi's confidence, expansiveness, body language, emotion, and voice worked together in a way that communicated something much bigger than any of those parts alone could have done.

Ravi's example gave me a vision for how a person's voice and speech could be united behind an idea in a way that I had rarely seen in the theater. What I saw in Ravi was more than a man who spent a lot of time getting his content right. Granted, it takes an amazing amount of work to do that preparation, and it is essential to good communication, but from watching Ravi on that day (and on subsequent occasions), I discovered that good preparation is only the minimum requirement and basic necessity for allowing the Holy Spirit to *begin* his work. A sermon, talk, or performance reaches a point where it is no longer a speech. It becomes far more dynamic. The audience listens and communes with the speaker as one collective mind, and there is a holy moment of inspiration and conviction that goes beyond logic or emotional impression. Moments like these are divine.

Ravi's model was of someone not satisfied with simply having good content. He wanted to make sure that the ideas were expressed vigorously so that the audience would feel the full weight of his message. He demonstrated that the voice was the channel or instrument for this to happen. It isn't enough to simply get the words right. If Ravi's vocal instrument was not up to the challenge of physically delivering the full expression and weight of the message God had given him, then it would not be complete. It may be communicating truth but not the fullest range of spirit. Jesus tells us that God wants worshipers "in spirit and truth" (John 4:23). That is the goal. And our vocal instrument is one important part of God's magnificent body that helps us get there.

An Unexpected Break

These experiences encouraged me to begin studying the Bible more closely and eventually led me to enroll in seminary. I chose Alliance Theological Seminary, just north of New York City, where Ravi Zacharias was a professor. I went to seminary with a desire to serve God, but I wasn't exactly sure how I would do it!

While I was attending seminary, Ravi discovered that I had a theatrical background and he encouraged me to use my drama skills as a ministry. At that time, drama in churches was just starting to get some attention, but it was mostly as a way of illustrating sermons with sketches and short skits. I wasn't motivated to go in that direction.

Rather, the Lord inspired me to do something different. I began asking, "Why not use the skills and techniques developed from acting and the theater, integrate it into what I have learned from preachers and teachers, and apply all of that into word-for-word dramatic presentations of the Bible?"

I had gone to seminary to serve the Lord, uncertain with whether I was being called to serve in a pastoral ministry. Like most people in seminary, I had a passion to know God and to share God with others. Now I was finding that the act of reading the text was itself a homily to the congregation. Maybe that was my calling?

> The act of reading the text was itself a homily to the congregation.

Shortly after Ravi's encouragement to use drama in ministry, someone invited me to lead one of our seminary chapels. I gave a little talk and then presented the first two chapters of Mark's gospel from memory. It was a seventy-three-verse monolog that I prepared, using my skills as an actor, and I wanted people to experience Jesus in a fresh way.

Similar to my first Scripture reading experience at church, the response of the students and faculty was strong. The seminary in those days had a bit of a conformist culture. A few students thought what I was doing in worship was peculiar, but lots of people gave me feedback and it was all compelling. I was encouraged to continue pursuing this unique ministry. I began to memorize the entire book of Mark—almost 15,000 words. It took months of preparation and rehearsal, but I was finally ready.

I reserved a big lecture hall at adjoining Nyack College for four consecutive weekends. I billed it as a dramatic performance of the Bible—"The Gospel according to Mark, as told by Max McLean." The date was September 1983.

Among the people in the audience on one of those nights were Warren and Michelle Bird. Warren was a new seminary student with something of a journalistic bent. We struck up a friendship that has lasted through the years, eventually leading to articles that he has written about me in Christian magazines (and now to this book-with-DVD that you are reading).

Another member in the audience was Rev. Dahl Seckinger, the Christian and Missionary Alliance district superintendent for the New York metro area. He told me that he and his wife, Joyce, were just stunned by the experience. Dahl proceeded to write every pastor in the district, urging them to invite me to their church. Soon after that performance, I was traveling around to churches, presenting Mark's gospel dramatically, word for word, with no prop other than a stool.

The first church to put me on an airplane (April 1984) was Ward Presbyterian in Livonia, Michigan. They brought me out to do Mark's Gospel, which typically ran just under two hours (with an intermission after Mark 9:1), and I found that the readings were consistently well received.

The modest honorariums that came from my performances covered only a small portion of our family expenses, not to mention my seminary tuition. My day job was with the National Religious Broadcasters (NRB), headquartered near our home. I sold advertising for the trade magazine sponsored by the NRB.

My job required me to attend the annual NRB conventions. In 1984, I was invited to give my first Scripture reading at NRB, and I was asked to return for another reading in 1987. That was the year I began seriously going on the road with my presentations.

But things really took off in 1994, when several people, including Norman Plunkett of Peachtree Media, encouraged me to get involved in radio. "If you could do a one-, two- or three-minute Scripture reading, radio stations will pick it up," Norm advised.

Norm opened the door for me, but I still had to fund it! Two years earlier, I had founded Fellowship for the Performing Arts (FPA), an organization to support the work of expressing faith through the dramatic arts. At the time I was on the road around 150 to 200 nights a year, and it was a tough way to live. But I was motivated to continue fulfilling the vision God had called me to. By starting FPA I could now raise support, put myself on salary, and be more strategic in fulfilling my vision.

One of the first things we did through FPA was to produce the NIV New Testament. That effort has since grown into the Listeners Bible line of products in the English Standard Version (ESV), King James Version (KJV), and New International Version (NIV) translations. My daily radio program, *Listen to the Bible,* has since grown to almost seven hundred affiliates worldwide. The other thing FPA allowed me to do was to produce Mark's gospel, and subsequently to expand my performances to the Acts of the Apostles, Genesis, and Philippians in fully produced theatrical settings. I have collaborated with other artists to present John and Revelation as well.

My love for great Christian literature led me to record and release *Classics of the Christian Faith*—a series of audio recordings that includes *The Conversion of Saint Augustine* (from Book 8 of his *Confessions*), Martin Luther's *Here I Stand*, John Bunyan's *The Pilgrim's Progress*, Jonathan Edward's *Sinners in the Hands of an Angry God*, George Whitfield's *The Method of Grace,* and William Wilberforce's *Real Christianity.* The idea of this series is to introduce these extraordinary works to a contemporary audience.

Most recently, I produced a stage adaptation of C. S. Lewis's *The Screwtape Letters* that opened Off Broadway in New York City in 2007, and has since moved to Washington, D.C., and Chicago, with other cities yet to come. In 2009 *Christianity Today* did a feature article about it.[1]

Most important, I continue to present God's Word in dramatic ways. Not long ago, theater critics reviewed a presentation of Mark's Gospel for the *Chicago Tribune* and the *Chicago Sun-Times.* Here in part is what they wrote:

> With wit and humor Max McLean brings a dramatically rooted clarity to what is a profoundly mysterious odyssey.
>
> Hedy Weiss, *Chicago Sun-Times*

> Whatever your interest in the life of Jesus...there's nothing like experiencing the events of this earth-shattering life at one sitting...Max McLean refuses to upstage the narrative...letting the words and vivid biblical characters have their say...Life-changing moments come from the text.
>
> Chris Jones, *Chicago Tribune*

LOOKING BACK

At the root of Christianity is the admission that this world is not what it ought to be, and at the heart of being a follower of Christ is the confession that "I am part of the problem." My vision, as I read and perform, is to select portions from the Bible and the treasury of Christian literature that help people to recognize their predicament and to move them toward a more humble understanding of themselves and a closer relationship with God. For the theater, my vision is to select stories that explore how and why consequential choices are made, and then to produce those stories in a manner that engages diverse audiences.

The first time I presented the Bible as a dramatic reading, the impact was immediate and profound. Since that time, God has provided me with opportunities to present the Bible to people of all ages, across the religious and cultural spectrum, through live presentations, on radio, and on television to hundreds of thousands — perhaps millions of people.

You may find it interesting to know that in my daily devotional reading of the Bible, I do not read out loud. Most of my private devotional life is spent silently reading, studying, and journaling. These devotional times are rooted in a desire to listen to God and to receive. However, when I do longer segments of the Bible, reading them aloud does help me engage the text more than just silently reading. I try not to think about my reading abilities or work on my delivery unless I am preparing for a public read or memorizing a passage.

The Bible Is Its Own Evangelist

In my travels and at many of my performances, I am often asked how I came to have this ministry of presenting the Bible dramatically. That's one reason I am putting my story in this chapter. Drama, theater, and storytelling are the mediums God has used in my life to fulfill my desire to make Christ known.

On that day, years ago, when I heard those verses from Galatians and a few days later read the gospel of John in one sitting, I saw the sacrificial love of Jesus and I responded. I instantly knew that Jesus' death on the cross and his resurrection were of supreme importance to me personally. I knew, after reading the Bible, that I would never again be the same. But it wasn't until later, when I sat under teachers and professors, that I was able to explain what had happened to me.

> Drama, theater, and storytelling are the mediums God has used in my life to fulfill my desire to make Christ known.

I had a similar experience the first time I read the book of Genesis. The hugeness and audacity of the first book of the Bible are simply overwhelming. Genesis is filled with massive personalities, people who made an extraordinary impression on me. But what really struck me as I read was how God interacted with each of them personally. Genesis showed me how God involves himself in our lives, directing the course of events to a particular purpose for his glory and our ultimate good.

What motivates me to memorize books of the Bible, like Mark, Genesis, and the Acts of the Apostles? Why do I rehearse, over and over again, to present them dramatically? My work and ministry are rooted in a deep desire to recapture and share those powerful initial experiences I had with the God of the Bible. In my presentation of God's Word, I want others to capture something of my own personal experience. I want others to come to know what I have found to be true. In the words of my pastor, Tim Keller, "Although I am more sinful and weaker than I ever imagined, in Christ I am more loved and accepted than I ever dared to hope."

My dramatic readings are also motivated by the examples and directives in the Bible itself for it to be read aloud—as we explore in chapter 3. In fact, scholars note that Bible reading in ancient times was dramatic, and so my public readings recreate elements of what people in first-century culture would have experienced.[2]

The Bible is its own evangelist. I came to faith because I was deeply affected by the words of the Bible. The famous British preacher Charles Spurgeon was once asked how he responded to criticisms of the Bible. "Very easy," he responded. "I defend the Bible the same way I defend a lion. I simply let it out of its cage." That quote captures our vision for this book and for the growth of ministries that are committed to the passionate, articulate, and powerful reading of Scripture. Isn't it time to let the Bible out of the cage, or (to borrow from the title of this book) to unleash God's Word?

When I tell a Bible story, I have a quiet confidence that God is going to do a mighty work by the very act of reading his Word. Therefore, my objective is to engage hearers and draw them into the Word of God. My role is to use my skills and abilities, as best I can, to draw them into an experience with the Word.

I remember a discussion I once had with a lighting designer. In the course of our interchange I asked him, "If you died tonight, would you go to heaven?" His answer surprised me: "I used to think so until I started working with you." He explained that in listening to the performance he had heard the message of the gospel in a way he had never heard before. He came to understand his need for a Savior, a need he had never truly realized before. That need led to an intimate discussion about Jesus and his grace. He believed and trusted in what Jesus did for him on the cross.

From time to time we get letters or emails that tell us, "I came to faith because of listening or seeing your presentation of the Bible." Others say, "That verse you spoke today on the radio really convicted me. I need to deal with that." When I read through these, I continually remember that this is not about me; it's the Word of God doing its powerful work in people's hearts.

In Romans 10:17, we read that "faith comes from hearing the message, and the message is heard through the word of Christ." This passage is foundational to the idea of reading Scripture aloud. Faith comes as a result of people receiving a message that has been spoken, and that message is Jesus Christ expressed through the words of the Bible. In Galatians 4:20, Paul writes to the church, "How I wish I could be with you now and change my tone." Paul knows that as wonderful as a letter is, it would be even better for them to hear his voice so they can truly understand the energy and weight behind his words. The spoken word has the ability to communicate both content and emotion and is an essential means of delivering the truth about God.

> Our vision for this book: It's time to let the Bible out of the cage ... to unleash God's Word.

A well-written sermon can fail to carry the nuances of tone and emotion that come when the message is eventually preached. And the same is true when we simply read the Bible silently in our times of private devotion. A different level of insight emerges when we actually hear the Word read aloud. When the Bible is spoken well, it penetrates and enlivens the heart. Getting our hearts inside the text of Scripture requires a kind of "vocal exegesis." That's the ultimate goal of our Scripture reading—moving the content beyond the head into the heart of those listening.[3]

Before we get into the details of learning to read, it's important that we find the right people. While all of us can read the Bible and should seek to grow in our ability to read it with passion and emotional power, the ministry of reading the Word is also a gift that God gives to certain people in the body of Christ. In the next chapter, we will look at how to go about finding the right people to read the Scriptures and what steps to take to develop a ministry of Scripture reading in a local congregation.

Chapter Two

Recruiting Others Who Love the Game

—————————

I'M A SEASON TICKET HOLDER for the Rutgers University football team—the Scarlet Knights. I've watched firsthand the remarkable turnaround that occurred after Greg Schiano accepted the head coaching position in 2000. At the time it was ranked as one of the worst Division One football programs in the nation! Yet in 2006 Schiano was awarded several Coach of the Year honors for orchestrating what many considered to be one of the top turnaround stories in college football history, transforming the hapless Scarlet Knights into a consistent winner in the tough Big East Conference.

Schiano is a follower of Christ and speaks regularly to Christian groups in New Jersey. I recall an article describing how he recruits players for his team. When Schiano interviews a player's high school coach he asks, "Does your player love the game?" That's a make-or-break question for him. "If the coach blinks or wavers in the slightest degree, I won't recruit the player, no matter how talented he is," Schiano explained. He understands that if people don't love the game, they won't do the work necessary to be great. He knows that many people play well at the high school level simply by talent alone. But if they don't have the motivation to get better, they won't excel at the college level, where the stakes are higher.

Schiano aims to recruit only those who truly love the game. There's something to learn from that when recruiting for a Scripture reading ministry—or any volunteer enterprise. For football players, you want to know more than how much they can bench press, how fast they can run, or how agile they are. Those qualities are important, but even more essential are the final questions: Do they love the sport? Is it something they'll put energy into?

I certainly don't want to overstate the analogy. Division One football players are like gladiators, committing most of their waking hours to the sport. There's a huge difference between the commitment of time sought from a D–1 football player and from a volunteer Scripture reader. But the commitment of heart and attitude are surprisingly comparable.

When looking for the right Scripture readers, it's important to look for those with vocal skills and the ability to be comfortable in front of a crowd, but perhaps more important are Greg Schiano–style questions: Do they enjoy it? Is Scripture reading something they'll put energy into? Do they want to grow, mature, and improve in this particular ministry to the church? When I look for people to serve as readers at my church, if I don't spot a passion and desire to see the Bible come alive, I've learned that it's best to keep looking for other potential readers.

> Churches need people who will read Scripture with enthusiasm, conviction, and disciplined preparation.

Why would I pass over talented people, simply because they lack the passion? It's because the stakes are so high. If Scripture is the lifeblood of our faith, and we want to transfuse that to the congregation in a way that brings life and transformation, then churches need people who will read Scripture with enthusiasm, conviction, and disciplined preparation.

I believe God has put one or more people in every church who, like me, have been touched powerfully by the spoken Word, and, if given the opportunity to read publicly—or to develop a team of readers—will work at it with the same spirit as one of Greg Schiano's recruits!

> I believe God has put one or more people in every church who, like me, have been touched powerfully by the spoken Word.

An important verse for me in this context is Ephesians 2:10, "For we are God's workmanship, created in Christ Jesus to do good works, which God prepared in advance for us to do." The context of this verse is that we are saved by God's merciful grace for a purpose, namely, to serve the body of Christ in some way. Therefore he gives us an affinity, a heart to enjoy a particular work or ministry, along with the desire to develop it and become good and proficient in exercising that discipline.

NEEDING MORE GAME LOVERS

Willow Creek Community Church, located in the Chicago suburbs, is one of the largest and most influential churches in the country. The church, under the leadership of Bill Hybels, has been a pioneer in emphasizing a church-wide focus on "seekers": people who have not yet experienced a life-changing faith relationship with Jesus Christ.

In 2007, Willow Creek publicized the results of a research project called Reveal,[1] which caused quite a stir in the evangelical church world. Reveal began as Willow Creek's staff asked how well their church was doing at helping people move along a spiritual spectrum — from atheists (or any other beginning point) to becoming totally devoted followers of Christ. Their working assumption, which is true at most churches, was that church activity drives spiritual growth. They assumed that greater participation in small groups, worship services, and other activities was the best indicator that a person was growing spiritually.

To find out whether this view matched reality, they did a thorough survey of their sizable congregation. The survey asked people to indicate what helped them to grow or caused them to stall in their faith journey. It also asked people what helped, and didn't help, as they moved forward spiritually. Willow then offered subsequent versions of the survey to other churches across the country who wanted to assess their own congregations.

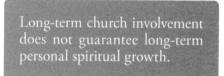

Long-term church involvement does not guarantee long-term personal spiritual growth.

Since that time, thousands of churches have been surveyed, and Willow Creek has documented that long-term church involvement does not guarantee long-term personal spiritual growth. The research has uncovered two major barriers to spiritual growth. The first barrier is what the Willow team describes as being spiritually "stalled." Virtually all people say that they've been stalled at some point in their spiritual development, including more than one out of five church attenders (23 percent) who reported that they are *currently* stalled in their spiritual growth. The second barrier, however, is the sense people have that their church is letting them down. These "dissatisfied" people are found across all segments of the spiritual continuum. Almost one out of five (17 percent) in the total sample are dissatisfied with the role their church plays in helping them grow spiritually.

People who were *not* stalled or dissatisfied credit the following as helping them grow and to take the next spiritual steps. Three of their top four responses indicated that their church had, in the words of the survey:

- helped me understand the Bible in greater depth
- helped me develop a closer personal relationship with Christ
- challenged me to grow and take the next step in my faith

How did that happen? It was clear from the responses that Bible *information* alone was not enough; people indicated that they grow through Bible *application*. They wanted more biblical content, including a more frequent use of Scripture throughout the worship service, but they also wanted help in learning how to apply and relate that content to their lives.

In response, Willow Creek and many other churches have begun changing their format. Worship services, even seeker-sensitive ones, are now offering additional Scripture readings, more personal prayer, and more challenging teaching from the Bible. The results of the Reveal study show us that people have a strong desire to dig deeply into God's Word, and the findings reinforce the idea that unleashing the Word of God is an essential key to ongoing spiritual growth.

The findings of the Reveal study have led churches to recognize that they haven't adequately exposed their people to Scripture, and many churches are seeking more engaging ways to involve people in Bible application. One hoped-for outcome of this study is that churches will begin to take the public reading of Scripture more seriously, positioning it more intentionally in worship services.

This means that churches are seeing the need for trained readers of Scripture is greater now than ever before. More and more people will need to step forward at their churches and offer to read Scripture as part of worship. Some churches may need to begin building and training a team of Scripture readers. We also hope that this renewed emphasis on the importance of Scripture will affect what happens at home as parents take more initiative to read the Bible aloud to their children and as couples spend time reading the Scriptures to one another.

BIRTH OF A SCRIPTURE READING TEAM

Redeemer Presbyterian in Manhattan, where Sharon and I are members, has always been a church that is friendly to skeptics, and yet the Bible is prominently emphasized. Our pastor, Tim Keller, and his preaching team unpack their messages with constant reference to the Bible. The three goals highlighted in the Reveal survey— "help me understand the Bible in greater depth, help me develop a closer personal relationship with Christ, and challenge me to grow and take the next step in my faith"— readily describe what we have been attempting to do. What's new for us, however, is the emergence of a Scripture reading group. The teaching pastor no longer reads the passage at the beginning of his sermon. Instead, we have developed and trained a group of gifted lay readers who read the Scripture passage each week just before the pastor delivers the sermon message.

I first organized our Scripture reading group back in 2002. It originally started as a "may I help?" conversation with our director of worship and arts after I had committed to Redeemer as a member. I introduced myself and offered to serve the church, if there was a place for my gifts to be used. We dialogued about it, and he began asking me to read the Scripture at occasional worship services. These initial readings were well received, and I eventually received permission to develop a team of readers to cover all Sunday-morning church services, year round.

In building the team, I initially sought recommendations for potential readers from church staff and members. To help launch the ministry, I was looking for some key people who had theater, radio, or broadcast experience and who had interest in using their skills to serve the church by reading the Scripture prior to the teaching.

After our initial lay readers program was established, we moved from personal recommendations to an audition-based approach, much like you would for vocal soloists, musicians, or other worship ministries that require specialized ability.

> The greatest compliment we receive happens when people say, "After hearing the Scripture, I really look forward to hear the teaching."

The response to the reading ministry has been wonderful. We regularly receive positive and affirming comments about our readings. In many ways, the greatest compliment we receive happens when we read the Scripture and people say, "After hearing the Scripture, I really look forward to hear the teaching." Recently, *Leadership Journal*, a magazine for pastors and church leaders, recognized our team at Redeemer as a model for other churches in this arena as it featured a short article about our reading group.[2]

SKILL NECESSARY, NOT JUST HEART

Manhattan is a city filled with actors, so I knew that some of our church members would have some background in voice and oral interpretation. I reasoned that it made sense to build the group by recruiting the "voice professionals" in the church, particularly those who could deliver the text with pathos, humility, and insight and could thus take the Scripture reading segment in the worship service to even higher levels. For those who aren't located in a major metropolitan area, it may make sense to look for people with skills in broadcasting, singing, teaching, sales, or community theater. You don't need to be a professional to read well. People with *any* background who are known as gifted storytellers should be on your list of potential candidates for the team.

> People with *any* background who are known as gifted storytellers should be on your list of potential candidates for the team.

I am convinced that selection is 90 percent of the process, and so I always take the auditions very seriously, seeking people in the congregation who have both strong skills and a healthy attitude for service. I look for giftedness, character, and commitment. I am not afraid to ask people if they are members. If not, I ask them if they are willing to go through the membership process or if they are involved in our church's small group ministry. On many of these occasions my questions have prompted candidates to examine their own commitment to our church, and they have ended up becoming more engaged and involved through this ministry. It's important to me and to our worship pastor that the reader has made a commitment to the church and is prepared to serve the congregation in this way. In addition, I listen carefully for a good understanding of the meaning of the text and some kind of emotional connection, but not an overly dramatic reading.

When readers do their work properly, they are "pre-preaching." Good Scripture readings set up the emotional and intellectual connection that a reader has to the text. Readers help the congregation begin forming questions about the text and encourage them to anticipate how the teaching pastor will address a particular issue.

> When readers do their work properly, they are "pre-preaching."

As I am recruiting, I also take the time to spell out a list of responsibilities for the reader position. This includes a rough approximation of how often they will be expected to read (every six or seven weeks for a one-year period), the need for them to download an early draft of the bulletin (typically by Wednesday), which lists the Bible text to be read, and the requirement that they spend at least thirty minutes rehearsing the text and arrive early to the service. Readers are also responsible to have a back-up plan in case of illness or unexpected travel.

For the audition, I ask the reader to read the assigned text aloud at least eight times. After eight readings, they will have a good sense of the text, so strong that it will almost seem as if they have it memorized.

Ellie Ellsworth has been a reader at Redeemer for four years. When she prepares her reading, she tries to move beyond a simple monolog. "I don't focus on words so much as an interchange," she says. "I picture myself in a dialog with my peers, perhaps talking to my dear friend who was in trouble a month ago. It's less like a pushing out words and more like a conversation."

At the same time she tries to prepare by simulating the exact experience. "I hold or place the paper I'll be reading from exactly the way I'll do it at church," she says. That helps her not sound "readery," as she calls it. "I need to know the text well enough that I'm available to what's going to happen: to the people, to the Holy Spirit, and to the word being spoken."

LOOKING FOR INFLECTION

When I read, I also go over the text multiple times. I think about how I will phrase the line so I can determine my inflection: the way I change my pitch or the loudness of my voice as I read a particular word or phrase. In my readings, getting the right inflection is one of the essential keys to communicating the meaning of the text. The proper inflection helps me find the emotional undertow within the text. It connects the passage more viscerally to the congregation. While we certainly want hearers to connect at the head level, understanding the meaning of each thought block in the text, we also want them to go deeper and gain an understanding of the author's motivation and intent at that moment.

I especially take time to study the verbs in the sentence. People tend to hear and "see" action. Verbs move the story forward. When readers take the time to explore the verbs within a passage (see pages 75–76), they often discover keys that unlock how to read the narrative. In my preparation, playing with the verbs, reciting them in different ways, is essential. Of course, all this prep work must be hidden when it comes time to actually present the text. The background "spade work" that a reader does makes the actual delivery during worship more interesting, alive, and engaging.

> Verbs move the story forward.

Steve Shaffer, another reader, draws attention to the importance of remembering your listeners and what it is like to hear the passage, not just read it. "An effective reader helps people process one thought at a time," Steve says, affirming that readers must "listen to the audience." When we are engaged in a conversation, we are attuned to whether or not the other parties are "getting it"—do they understand what we are saying? If they are, we feel like it is a good conversation. If they do not understand us, the interchange can feel flat or boring, since there is no connection between the speaker and the listener.

When people are engaged with what you are saying, it is because they are tracking with you "one thought at a time." They are getting it. They are using an active ear as you speak. Good speaking involves looking at the message from the perspective of the listener. How can my reading encourage good listening?

TRANSFORMING THE READER

Getting to the point of engagement means that each reader in our group should be personally impacted by the text. Reader David Plant comments, "I know I get more out of the reading than others do from my reading it. I get to spend extra time pouring over what's being said, thinking about the author's point of view, and looking for the 'why' for the words being said. By the time I read it at church, it's really rich for me."

Actively reading the text multiple times makes a reader well primed for the sermon. As reader Elizabeth Davis says, "It's like taking a shovel and digging deeper into the nutrients of the Word." She finds added personal meaning as she practices her reading out loud, "allowing the Holy Spirit to have his way in my own life as I encounter the passage," she says. "When the Bible is read aloud with emotion and conviction appropriate to the context, infused with the fact that this is what we base our lives upon, it's earth-shaking!"

Reader Catrina Ganey has likewise been personally transformed as she prepares. "It's been a humbling experience. In the beginning, all I thought about was me; I was terrified that I would stumble or mispronounce a word. Then I realized it is about Jesus. My goal became, 'I want them to see Jesus when I read the Word. Were they ushered into His presence?' As the Bible says, 'He must become greater; I must become less'" (John 3:30).

SCRIPTURE PRESENTATION AS MINISTRY

Even though we've supplied readers for many years now, we continue to receive great feedback. Senior pastor Tim Keller is our most frequent teaching pastor. He even observed that this team of gifted volunteers has helped him protect his voice over time. "I preach four times a Sunday. The team reads better than I do, and it saves twelve minutes on my voice!"

Over time, the personalities and styles of the various readers also come through. In fact, when an assisting pastor from Redeemer traveled to a country where Christians cannot meet openly, he discovered a group of Christians who had been downloading the church's sermons for several years, playing them in their house church meetings. "They wanted to know about the readers," the pastor reported. "They felt as if they had come to know them through listening to the weekly recordings."

This regular pattern of strong reading has also continued to raise the congregation's expectations, heightening the readers' awareness that their potential bobbles and stumbles or even lack of passion will be noticed and can draw attention away from the content.

What keeps the weekly reading segment in the worship service from lapsing into a performance? "A good reading invites listeners into the text," says Tom Jennings, director of worship and arts. "A performance draws attention merely to the skill of the artist but not the content of their art. A thoughtful, clear, considered reading brings to life material that has, after all, been passed down in oral form for most of the church's history." As reader Catrina Ganey says, "We serve a vibrant and exciting God! Why should reading Scripture be any less than vibrant, exciting, and with a powerful sense of truth and understanding?"

When I hear comments like that, I'm eager to share our insights with other church leaders and encourage them to elevate the quality of the Scripture reading segment in their worship services as well. In fact, there are many areas of church ministry that could benefit from the public reading of Scripture—from youth groups to home schooling sessions, from church board meetings to parent-to-child or spouse-to-spouse reading at home. There are many untapped opportunities for the Bible to be fully unleashed among the people of God.

When I was at seminary, Ravi Zacharias (introduced in chapter 1) noticed my skills in theater and took the initiative to encourage it in ministry. Ravi saw that I "loved the game," that I had a gift, and that I wanted to serve. Ravi has an evangelistic heart and is always looking for new ways to articulate the gospel. I was greatly encouraged by his words and blessed that he noticed my gifts and sought to nurture them.

There are probably several people in every congregation who "love the game" of reading the Scriptures and would be greatly encouraged if someone were to seek them out. What is the reading of the Bible like in your church? Do the Scripture readings feel flat and uninteresting? When Scripture reading is done well, it adds spiritual nourishment and positive excitement to worship. It will provide lasting benefits, both to those Christians who have made a commitment to Jesus as well as to skeptics or those dissatisfied with their faith journey.

Chapter Three

No Longer the Worst Moment

When Sharon and I first started attending church together, I remember my initial response during worship. Week after week the same thing would happen at a particular point in the service. The pastor would begin his message by introducing his topic, and then he would read the Bible passage for the day.

I would significantly engage with what he was saying only after he had actually begun to teach. During the reading, I tuned out. As soon as he was finished with the biblical text, I would think to myself, "Now we get to the good part." I loved to hear him *preach* the Word far more than *read* the Word.

I've heard a lot of good preaching in my life. And I believe our present pastor is one of the best teaching pastors, if not *the* best, both in content and delivery style, that I've ever heard. But great communicators often preach far better than they read aloud. Do you wonder why that's true? Most likely, during the hours and hours they spend preparing, they read the Bible passage repeatedly — but silently to themselves. They pray. They draw from their classroom training at seminary or Bible college and think about how to interpret and apply the Bible. They make written notes of what they're going to say. They may bounce ideas off of others and practice their message aloud.

Then, at the appointed moment, they tap into a skill that they've used all their lives: they talk. They may be more passionate, expressive, or dramatic than in ordinary conversation, but for many it's a communication style that's as natural and comfortable as talking or breathing.

So why is the *reading* of the Bible so flat, when many preachers are gifted communicators? The answer is that the dynamics of reading and speaking are totally different. Reading from a page represents a different skill set than speaking impromptu or from prepared notes.

> Reading from a page represents a different skill set than speaking impromptu or from prepared notes.

Chances are pretty good that most preachers haven't spent time practicing reading the Scripture passage out loud. In addition, they've probably never had training in reading aloud, and they may have never seen it done well.

A MEMORABLE DIFFERENCE

I remember attending a church one Sunday in Dallas several years ago. I had been brought there to give a dramatic presentation of Genesis. I had done the performance the evening before, and I was now attending worship services at the church before flying home.

Just before the pastor gave his message, a lay reader presented the Scripture passage of the day. Whoa! His reading grabbed my attention. The entire congregation was deeply engaged. The reader walked confidently, but humbly, to the pulpit and in a deep powerful voice articulated the sense of the passage in a magnificent way. The passage itself was powerful. The delivery was patient but expressive. The voice quality was pure and strong. I found his reading as worshipful and as engaging as the choir anthem that had preceded it. In fact, the combination of beautiful music and his powerful reading of the Bible was almost sublime. I heard someone in the congregation whisper, "We don't need a sermon."

Now as much as I enjoyed the reading, that person was wrong. Of course a powerful reading is not intended to replace the sermon message; it is done to prepare the congregation to engage with the message. The congregation on that morning was more prepared to listen and engage with the sermon than they had been before. The Scripture reading raised their expectation level, creating anticipation for the message.

I knew that the minister of worship at that church had a background in the dramatic arts, and he had a vision to help his people emotionally connect with the Bible through reading Scripture aloud. He had carefully selected people from the congregation who had both a heart for the Scriptures and the skill to read. I found out that the person who read that morning was a professional singer, a voice teacher, and owas a respected member of the congregation. He had combined his talent and spiritual passion, blended them with some quality rehearsal time, and brought them to bear on the passage.

> Scripture reading doesn't need to be the low point or even the ho-hum transition point of worship.

Scripture reading doesn't need to be the low point or even the ho-hum transition point of worship. It can speak powerfully to people and build an eagerness to hear what the pastor is going to say.

The third section of this book will help you learn to do just that. As my pastor, Tim Keller, says in his endorsement to the book, "In most church services the reading of the Word is poorly and hurriedly done. What a missed opportunity! The public reading of God's Word is an interpretive act that takes skill and thought and has historically been understood as a means of grace equal with preaching and sacraments."

Rethinking Why People Get Asked to Read Scripture

Another reason we have dull, lifeless readings of Scripture is because of the way people are selected to read. Too often their selection occurs because of their role in church. "Now one of our elders will read from Genesis 47:1 – 7." In this case, the choice of readers had zero bearing on their training or ability. We usually don't do that for other aspects of the worship arts — "Now one of our elders will sing" or "paint" or "edit a video" or "do a mime." There is a night-and-day difference when you compare a trained Scripture reader with readers who are neither skilled nor practiced, regardless of their title or position in the church.

> Asking someone to read the Scripture in worship is not the best way to make a statement that "this person is a leader."

Asking someone to read the Scripture in worship is not the best way to make a statement that "this person is a leader." Readers should have a certain level of skill and pathos with their material, the same way musicians or other artists do when they contribute to the worship experience.

Sadly, most readers, whether lay volunteers or staff at the church, are often recruited without much thought or intentionality. They are chosen largely because of convenience or proximity. The pastor may call Jim the deacon to ask how the food pantry is going. At the end of his conversation he might add, "By the way, I'm teaching from Romans 8:1–5 this weekend; would you do the reading?" Or a reader is chosen after a hallway conversation at church: "Thanks for that update on the missions trip, and, as long as we're chatting, would you mind doing the reading from Romans at this morning's services?" One of the first steps to improving the ministry of Scripture reading at your church is to be more intentional about the way you recruit and choose your readers.

> One of the first steps to improving the ministry of Scripture reading at your church is to be more intentional about the way you recruit and choose your readers.

They Mean It as a Compliment

When I read the Bible aloud at church, whether it's my own church or I'm visiting somewhere, I appreciate it when people say kind words to me afterwards. I feel somewhat embarrassed, however, when they say something like, "I didn't know the Bible could sound like that," or, "You really made the Bible come alive." They mean it as a compliment, and I thank them for it. Why are memorable readings of Scripture so rare that people feel a need to single it out? Certainly, there are other disciples just like me who have gifts and passions suitable for reading Scripture aloud. How can they become readers in their churches?

I went to drama school in England and trained in what's called "received pronunciation." To the American ear it makes speech sound heightened—a bit like I'm doing Shakespeare. That does make my readings sound distinctive, but the fact remains—too many churchgoers seem to lack any exposure to a vital, engaging, stimulating experience of hearing the Bible read well.

My collaborative writer, Warren Bird, recalls the first time he heard me read a section of Scripture. He was at the national conference of the Christian and Missionary Alliance denomination, chatting between sessions with a pastor in the back of the big meeting room. The buzz at those gatherings is a bit like the fellowship hall of a church — noisy and full of enjoyable conversation. Typically, when the next service starts, the noise will gradually wind down as people finish up and filter back into their seats.

But something else happened that day. Warren recalls a sudden and dramatic drop in the audience volume. He and his friend abruptly stopped their conversation and looked toward the front of the room to see what had happened. All they heard was a man's voice. Was someone making an important announcement? Was some unexpected news afoot?

No, it turns out that voice was mine. I was reading the Bible. It was a passage from Acts, but it stood out so much to Warren that he still remembers it to this day.

The truth is that it *was* an important announcement: it was God's Word to us! Shouldn't the reading of God's sacred text have the same impact on our minds and hearts as someone alerting us to breaking news or letting us know about an important change in the scheduled events of the day?

Low Expectations

I think it would be fair to say that most churches have pretty low expectations when it comes to the reading of the Bible in worship. My sense is that in most churches, worshipers don't *expect* to hear the Scriptures read with enthusiasm or preparation. In fact, I suspect that the generally accepted level of Scripture reading is such that it becomes a frequent lull or tune-out time. The quality bar at too many churches is set low, and no one seems to be challenging it.

Perhaps the reason is because we've all become so used to life in the desert that we cannot imagine what it would be like to experience the Promised Land. Low-quality reading is the norm in far too many churches, and many leaders lack imagination (and faith) for what could happen if gifted storytellers were to employ their skill sets in service to the church.

> The quality bar at too many churches is set low, and no one seems to be challenging it.

One Sunday years ago, I told my wife, Sharon, that I sometimes get upset if the worship service is dull and boring. It just seems wrong for us to leave church with an attitude of disengagement, tedium, and a sense of relief that says we're glad it's done.

Contrast that experience to worship services I've attended where, immediately following the benediction, the church auditorium explodes with energy emanating from the joy of worshiping with a community of believers who have heard the gospel preached "with a demonstration of the Spirit's power" (1 Corinthians 2:4). Every element of the worship service, from the music to the prayer and Scripture reading, is done as if it were the most important thing in the world.

> You do have a touch of the resurrected life, and I think that's what worship is about.

This critique isn't about worship styles or the type of music you prefer (my personal preference is more toward traditional hymns and liturgy). Rather, it's a wake-up call to those of us responsible for setting the direction of worship in our churches. I consider it a dereliction of duty to simply throw together a worship service in a cavalier, comewhat-may fashion where the music has no sense of flow and the pastor is unprepared.

But when God is affirmed and magnified through the sacred text and other vibrant expressions of faith, I come away inspired and changed. I find that I love people more, that the fellowship is sweeter, and that I am emboldened in my daily walk with the Lord to serve him. Jesus empowers me, enlivens me, and fills me with joy.

> When God is magnified through sacred text, I am emboldened in my daily walk with the Lord to serve him. God is the most fascinating, creative, energetic being in the entire universe.

That's the difference between leaving a service erupting with energy or fading out the door. God is the most fascinating, creative, energetic being in the entire universe. How can we allow worship to be boring?

Examples from Scripture

Over the years, I've recorded in their entirety three different translations of the Bible (I've recorded one translation twice).[1] As I prepared for these recordings, working my way through each of the Bible's roughly

1,200 chapters and 31,000 verses, I found several spots where people in these narratives were doing exactly what I was trying to do: reading Scripture aloud. I was fascinated by many of these passages.

For example, the book of Nehemiah tells the fascinating story of a great spiritual revival that occurred in Jerusalem. After the city's wall was rebuilt, everyone came together for a sacred assembly, and a gifted teacher named Ezra read the Book of the Law "aloud from daybreak till noon ... in the presence of the men, women and others who could understand. And all the people listened attentively" (Nehemiah 8:3). Others also read the Scripture and explained its relevance, "making it clear and giving the meaning so that the people could understand what was being read" (8:8). The people's hearts were touched; they "bowed down and worshiped the Lord with their faces to the ground" (8:6). They also began "weeping as they listened to the words of the Law" (8:9).

The prophet Amos prophesied, " 'The days are coming,' declares the Sovereign Lord, 'when I will send a famine through the land—not a famine of food or a thirst for water, but a famine of hearing the words of the Lord" (Amos 8:11). The people of Nehemiah's time had been experiencing such a famine. We may be too.

When Scripture reading is done well, it adds spiritual nourishment and intensifies the worship experience! We see this happening with Ezra and the people. As the Word is being read, the people are struck with conviction, their hearts are touched, and their emotions are engaged with the words they are hearing. The Lord used his Word during the time of Ezra to draw the people closer to himself, calling them to repentance.

This example isn't unusual. During times of genuine worship God's children have always listened for God's voice and responded. This is the essence of worship. The story of God and his interaction with men and women like Joseph, Abraham and Sarah, Moses, Job, Esther, and many others are more than just stories. They have been received by the church as the written, inspired, and sacred Word of God for thousands of years.

> During times of genuine worship God's children have always listened for God's voice and responded.

The Scriptures were meant to play a key role in homes, in community-wide religious assemblies, and eventually in the weekly worship services that became the local synagogues (see Acts 18:4).

During Jesus' time, synagogue worship included reading aloud a passage of Scripture from the book we now call the Old Testament. The reader could be a layperson, as we see in the story of Jesus, when he served as the reader at the Nazareth synagogue (Luke 4:16–21). The text specifically tells us that Jesus read from a scroll, but from other parts of the Gospels, we also know that Jesus memorized huge amounts of Scripture, evidenced by the way he quotes from twenty-four Old Testament books and by the way people respond to him, saying, "How did this man get such learning without having studied?" (John 7:15). By the age of thirty, Levites (those engaged in temple service) had to memorize the first five books of our Bible (which are more words than our entire New Testament) and be ready to quote them back verbatim in order to work in the temple.

When the New Testament church was born, Jesus' disciples met at least weekly for worship, both in large public gatherings and in homes (Acts 2:46; 20:20; 1 Corinthians 16:1). These gatherings often included readings or quotations from the Old Testament, or possibly an apostle's recounting of Jesus' teachings and the miracles he performed. Some of these recollections may have existed in written form and eventually became the foundation for the four Gospels.

In fact, the apostle Paul indicated in several places that his letters—the epistles that make up a large part of the New Testament—should be read aloud when the church gathered (Colossians 4:16; 1 Thessalonians 5:27). Another New Testament writing even invites God's blessing on the person who reads it to the congregation, as well as those who hear it and apply it to their hearts (Revelation 1:3). The few New Testament references to the actual worship of the early church indicate that worship frequently involved reading Scripture from the psalms or quoting from the teachings of Jesus and the apostles.

EXAMPLES FROM CHURCH HISTORY

Just as we saw the importance of Scripture reading in the Old Testament, you find a similar pattern of reading Scripture in the life of the early church. The New Testament is full of examples of people reading or quoting the Scriptures of their day—our Old Testament. The next time you read the gospel of Matthew, take notice of how many times Jesus quotes the Old Testament. Or try to count how many times the writer of Hebrews cites the Old Testament. If you want a real challenge, find every place in the letter of James that refers to a saying of Jesus.

The writings that became our New Testament were quickly incorporated into Christian worship. The writings of the early church father Justin Martyr, about AD 150, are the earliest accounts that refer to the specific role of Scripture reader. His *First Apology* (ch. 67) explains that "on the day called Sunday ... the memoirs of the apostles or the writings of the prophets are read as long as time allows. After the reader has finished, the presiding officer verbally instructs and exhorts us to imitate these shining examples." Later church writers also mention the idea of a designated Scripture reader (or lector) in worship.[2]

In fact, for thousands of years, from the earliest books of the Old Testament onward, the way most people experienced the Bible was not through the silent reading of the written Word—it was verbal. In fact, reading silently was almost unheard of in antiquity. Those who could not read or did not have access to the Bible would see and hear it from someone they knew. Sometimes the Bible was read from the written page, but often it was quoted from memory. Some scholars argue that early Christian authors wrote their inspired works anticipating that they would be not just read but performed publicly.[3] Until the invention of the printing press, people commonly memorized large portions of Scripture. A privileged few would sometimes read from the one Bible owned by their church. With the advent of printing technology, the Bible became a primary textbook for learning to read and an aid to public education.

CONCLUSION

I came across an interesting fact the other day. A normal person makes a decision about where to turn attention about 100,000 times a day. The brain is always drawn to *something*. This raises the question of how to make sure that when the Bible is read, that's what people are giving their attention to!

In this chapter, we've tried to suggest that the reading of Scripture in the church should be a high point for the service. Theologically, historically, and scientifically it makes sense that if we want people to truly engage the Word of God, we need to emphasize the act of reading the Scriptures.

John 4:23–24 tells us that the "kind of worshipers the Father seeks" are those who worship him "in spirit and truth." When I hear the Scriptures read intelligently, energetically, convincingly, and passionately, even the most familiar and shopworn texts draw me to a place where I can worship God in spirit and truth. This can happen at a Sunday morning church service, at a wedding or funeral, or even in home Bible studies, such as the one that led to my conversion.

If you're reading this book, you may have picked it up because you have both the heart and the talent to take Scripture reading to a new level. I hope you are convinced of the importance of this ministry and are excited about the possibilities for your church and ministry. The next section will show you that there are many contexts in which Scripture reading can happen, and then we will walk you personally through the mechanics of good reading.

CHAPTER FOUR

THE 9 PERCENT ISOLATION FACTOR

THE MESSAGE OF THIS CHAPTER can be summed up in one sentence: if 90 percent of effective Scripture reading comes from selecting gifted, trained, committed readers who "love the game" (chapters 2 and 3), another 9 percent of the unleashing process comes from isolation—making Scripture reading a separate element of the worship experience. By isolating the moment the Scripture is read, we enhance its power.

Certainly, offering a change of scene in the service does not, by itself, improve the reading of the Bible. If the reading is poor, then isolating it certainly won't help the situation. If you isolate something that's not all that good to begin with, you will only reinforce how bad it sounds. However, if the reading is effective and well executed, then isolating it in the

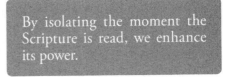

> By isolating the moment the Scripture is read, we enhance its power.

worship service will enhance its power and serve as an advertisement to the congregation that the Scripture is highly valued and its reading is an important part of our worship. The people, in turn, will be encouraged to devote more personal or small-group time to studying it in greater depth.

THE PROBLEM IS ONE OF BLURRING

Instead of making Scripture a separate and unique unit in the worship experience, many churches do what I call "blurring." It often unfolds like this: The person who has voiced the announcements shifts immediately into reading the Scripture passage. Or the teaching pastor will simply read the Scripture as part of the sermon message.

Both approaches fail to isolate the Scripture reading, and they therefore eliminate that special place in worship devoted exclusively to the reading of the Bible. When the reading of Scripture is simply incorporated into another part of the worship service, it loses significance. It's an invitation for people to hold off on their concentration until the reading is completed and the sermon begins.

I believe that this widespread practice of "blurring" has greatly contributed to the loss of impact, vitality, and power when reading Scripture in worship. The congregation sees the Scripture reading as a transitional time in the service and tunes it out, treating it as if it is part of the announcement routine; they tune back in only once the sermon has begun.

BENEFITS OF NOT BLURRING

What are some better alternatives? Let me illustrate some examples with Warren's friend Lisa, who has regularly read the Scripture in her Catholic congregation for years. "I have done it a hundred times, but I still have so much to learn," she recently commented. "I practice at home, but there is a lot to be aware of each time I read—how I stand, when to breathe, how to project my voice, whether I'm going too fast or too slow, and where I look!"

The Catholic church has isolated Scripture readings to the point that those who do it have a special name. Lisa is known as a *lector*, and she's part of a group of similar volunteers in her church parish. Catholic churches typically have a special place in their mass (worship service) for Scripture reading. For her parish there are four services each weekend, morning masses during the week, and various special Holy Day services. Each one requires a lector. In Lisa's church this involves about forty to fifty people throughout the year, and the lector schedule is set in four-month increments. Lisa reads once a month for the 9:30 Sunday morning mass, and she often substitutes for other masses when asked.

"For me, being a lector has provided a way to get closer to God and my faith," Lisa says. "Reading and studying Scripture has truly helped me understand it better and interpret it for my own daily life. I also have the hope as I read at church that someone who has been lost or distant from their faith is listening, and maybe one word, one reading, will touch them in a way that will heal or inspire them. The Word of God is awesome and amazing, and it can truly work through each one of us. Reading has given me many joyous moments, strengthened my public speaking ability, and most importantly brought me to a different level in my religious experience."

THE BLESSING STARTS WITH THE READER

Lisa's expression of serious responsibility and delight in serving well is a good example of what can happen to a reader. Scripture describes the blessing Lisa received this way: "How beautiful on the mountains are the feet of those who bring good news, who proclaim peace, who bring good tidings, who proclaim salvation, who say to Zion, 'Your God reigns!' " (Isaiah 52:7). The prophet was referring to the swift-running messenger who raced to the anxiously awaiting city of Jerusalem to announce that God had granted victory in battle and the land was now at peace.

Likewise, the heralds of today bring a much-needed word to an expectant people. The beauty of today's heralds lie not how quickly they can run, but in the skillful proclamation of God's Word, with energy, clarity, grace, and thoughtful expression. In Isaiah's sense of the word, those with "beautiful feet" are really those who rise, stand in the midst of their peers, and proclaim God's Word.[1]

Notice also that the herald whom Isaiah describes, while skilled, was not necessarily a Levite or priest (what we today refer to as a member of the clergy). Throughout the Bible we find examples of "laypeople" who are validated as public readers of God's Word.

One of the first mentioned was a king named Josiah. When the high priest found the book of God's law hidden in the temple, he presented it to King Josiah, who had a heart for God and was likely both skilled and experienced in public speaking. The king then gathered all the people of Jerusalem "from the least to the greatest. He read in their hearing all the words of the Book of the Covenant, which had been found in the temple of the LORD" (2 Kings 23:2). That day, the king became a beautiful messenger of God's Word as he read the written Word of God aloud in public worship.

THE BLESSING CONTINUES TO THE CONGREGATION

What I'm calling "the 9 percent isolation factor" does far more than bless the public reader of Scripture. It clearly helps elevate the role of Scripture reading for the entire congregation. The more isolated the Bible reading is in the worship service, the more it is taken seriously. And when Bible reading is taken seriously, greater effort and passion are given to it. When that happens, both the reader and the congregation will benefit.

Reader Model 1: Roster of Volunteers

Lisa's experience represents one of the more common approaches that churches use to isolate Scripture reading. The leaders of her church created a spot to be filled. Then they selected from a talented pool of readers who are committed to the process, train them, and build schedules to make sure the spot is filled effectively each week.

Catholic liturgy usually has three different Scripture readings at each Sunday mass, so the same reader typically covers all three. The readings change each week, so that most parts of the Bible are highlighted in a three-year cycle.

The training Lisa receives as a reader is typically divided into four different aspects.

Observation. Since Scripture reading occurs at each church service, she is regularly exposed to the reading of the Bible. She has seen a wide range of readings at her church, both good and bad. Some reads are lifeless, while others have an unnatural rhythm or an overly dramatic way of conveying the message, which can be distracting and at times even annoying. Yet others have such command and a sense of what the text is saying that it makes her want to sit on the edge of her pew as she anticipates each word. "I hope I help people sense the Bible's excitement and drama as I read," she says. Lisa has learned much about reading from personal observation, looking for good practices to copy and bad practices to avoid.

Guidebooks. Lisa's priest gives each of the lectors a guidebook that offers pronunciation aids, content understanding, and specific reading tips. For example, I opened one of the guidebooks to a reading from 1 Corinthians 1:3–9, which included these tips:

> Notice how the Apostle Paul changes his tone. Pause to have the assembly poised for the first-person address, which begins as a long and complex sentence. You need to understand its shifts and turns in order to proclaim it confidently.
>
> This final verse is key, so pause before it and proclaim it slowly, clearly, boldly, as a message of hope for your community.[2]

A book like this can be a goldmine of helpful guidance. That's also the intent of the book you're reading, and we have listed other resources like this in our bibliography.

Workshops. Lisa occasionally attends an area-wide training session known as "lector formation." It's sort of like a group workshop in which various speakers talk about the importance of Scripture reading and offer practical advice on public speaking.

Coaching. Lisa also gets informal feedback on her reading from her priest, from her fellow lectors, and from family members who attend that parish. "It's like having a coach, and I think I've gotten a lot better over the years," she says. In fact, one time her priest invited the readers to meet for a training session. Each had been videotaped while reading, and then the priest and another liturgy member reviewed it and gave

> Some readers have such command and a sense of what the text is saying that it makes the parishioners want to sit on the edge of their pew as they anticipate each word.

feedback. "I learned a lot about volume, whether we were speaking too quickly or quietly, and how often we looked up," says Lisa. "Some of us looked like bobbing heads!" She felt this was helpful feedback, even if it was difficult to watch.

Our Catholic friends have developed a strong system for Scripture reading in the decades since Vatican II, and they have learned to give attention and impact to the public reading of Scripture. They know that for most of the congregation, this is the primary way that people actually receive the words of the Bible.

These four ways of training readers—observing the model of others, using guidebooks, attending workshops, and being coached—can certainly be applied in any type of church.

Reader Model 2: Teamwork among Volunteers

Once you have committed to isolating the Scripture reading in your worship, you need a model for finding and developing your reader pool. A second model for developing Scripture readers places the emphasis on the leader for the Scripture team to provide coaching and encouragement. This model helps to develop a sense of team rather than merely a collection of individual players.

In chapter 2 I described the Scripture reading group at the church where Sharon and I are members. Once our church moved from "blurring" to isolating the Scripture reading, I committed to leading the group. Our team is more than a list of names on a schedule. In the beginning, we met together regularly. When we gathered together, I served as our facilitator, but we approached our time together with an attitude of peer learning. I had selected most of our readers because they had been identified by the leadership of our church as people with storytelling talents. Each person brought to the table training, experience, and skill in oral interpretation. Our challenge as a team was to figure out how to apply our talents and skills to fit our church's unique environment.

As we met together, our discussions were primarily about reminding everyone of the larger objective. Our goal was to elevate the Scripture passage on which the sermon teaching was based through careful interpretation and phrasing, bringing forth the meaning of the text with power and clarity.

Given that we were located in New York City, we wanted to provide a forum that would involve actors in particular, giving them an opportunity to use their skill set to contribute to our worship experience. Our discussion covered a wide range of topics, from the unique acoustics of the auditorium where we worship to how our gifts and skills best fit into the culture of our congregation. We didn't want to be so "over the top" that we drew attention to ourselves. Nor did we want to be so subdued that we shortchanged the impact of God's Word when read aloud.

We also gave each other feedback on our reading, much like any group of professionals might offer constructive, peer-to-peer feedback, sharing with one another how we could improve. We ended our time by asking each person to commit to the above objectives, to strive for excellence, to be available for an occasional rehearsal, and to help with any scheduling matters that might arise.

The team approach has such value to it that I'm surprised it's not done more often as a model for ministry. I have discovered over the years that anytime I did a project as part of a team, my work showed definite improvement, especially when experts on the subject or topic joined the conversation. Team members frequently challenged my assumptions and stretched my thinking. It's always better to work in community.

Reader Model 3: Double-Duty Musicians

Another way to isolate the Scripture reading and to develop Scripture readers in your church is to tap into the talent within the worship team or in your choir. If they are already engaged in some aspect of the worship service, it can be quite natural, at the appropriate time, for one of the worship team members to step forward to serve as reader. Sometimes, they can even weave the Scripture reading into worship by reading it in sections between various songs.

Musicians often have backgrounds where they have been trained in breathing, articulation, and phrasing. This is essential. They are skilled and committed to the church, and some readily demonstrate a "love for the game" (chapter 2), helping the Bible come alive in the hearts of those worshiping.

With some musicians, however, there may be a temptation to treat the Scripture like lyrics to a song, veering the text toward sentimentality and thus losing the potential edginess of a passage. So make sure that even when you recruit from your worship team or choir, you still do a thorough job of auditioning and training your readers.

Reader Model 4: Pastors Who Tag Team

Pastor A is preaching the message for the morning, so Pastor B does the reading before the sermon. This approach has the advantage of isolating the reading from the message, enabling the congregation to hear the text twice — once as a self-standing unit before the message, and then during the message perhaps in pieces or sections.

This model is a variation of the first three models. It is probably one of the simplest ways to introduce a new element in the reading of Scripture, but it depends heavily on the gifts and commitment of the pastors involved — and the willingness of that pastor to practice what Paul describes as one of the fundamental commitments of a minister: to "devote yourself to the public reading of scripture" (1 Timothy 4:13).

Reader Model 5: Readers Theater

Another way to isolate the reading — though done rarely, and if so, it should be entered into with caution — is for a group of readers to take the Scripture passage for the day and divide the speaking parts between a narrator and the various characters within the story. If the story describes a crowd — "and the people shouted" or "the congregation replied" or "the host of angels said" — then two or three people together could represent that part. Many sections of the Bible, from stories to dialog to poetry, readily lend themselves to a group reading approach.

Listening to multiple voices has merit, if well executed, in that it can bring a deeper perspective to a passage of Scripture. However, I would recommend this approach only if your church has appropriate talent and commitment. To do it well, dramatic readings of Scripture with multiple participants require a script writer, a director, numerous rehearsals, and additional technological issues (multiple microphones, etc.). Proceed with caution.

If the reading is under-rehearsed or executed poorly, it will detract from the power of the Scripture. The rule is that creativity should never supersede or blunt the message the Scripture is trying to convey. If it does not enhance the message, don't do it.

Reader Model 6: Responsive Reading

One way many churches isolate the reading is to have a moment in the service for the responsive reading. This occurs most commonly with "leader" and "people" parts and is a widespread practice in churches. The leader may be clergy or lay, depending on the church's tradition.

The strength of this reading style is that it allows everyone to participate and share in the experience. My primary concern with this model is that it forces the congregation to focus more effort on speaking in unison rather than on taking time to reflect on the words spoken. I fear the message of the text gets lost when this happens.

Furthermore, if the leader does not prepare or gives a flat reading, very little of the text's meaning is communicated. By contrast, a prepared leader, who takes the time to rehearse the passage in advance, can shape the reading's tone, mood, emotion, and sense of flow. But if the reader is that good, it may be best to read the entire passage solo rather than diverting their focus in order to read together in unison. Again, isn't the primary objective to find the best way to articulate the meaning of the Scripture to the congregation?

Reader Model 7: Singing or Chanting the Text

In some high-church liturgies, the Scripture is isolated by being sung or chanted, especially with the psalms. Chanting, also known as plainsong, is intoning the worship liturgy within a limited range of notes. In the Coptic liturgy, for example, selections from the following sections of Scripture are read in each weekly worship service:

1. A Pauline Epistle (one attributed to the Apostle Paul)
2. A Catholic Epistle (a non-Pauline epistle)
3. The Synaxarium (short biography of the Saint of the day)
4. The Gospels

Interestingly, the gospel reading is sung, while the other sections are read. All readings are done by laity, by those who have been ordained in their church as readers. In this tradition the Scripture reading has a special place in each service, and the reader is placed in an honored position. Yet I find that this rarely draws me to think about the meaning of the words; it only happens if done exceedingly well and if the format does not overwhelm the content. I am usually drawn to the melody or rhythm rather than the passage being sung. Yes, the reader is isolated and the Scriptures are given a place of honor in the service, but it is rare that it helps the congregation gain a better understanding or appreciation of the Bible

Unintentionally, many churches misapply the isolation factor we are advocating for reading Scripture. They use the Bible reading as a place of honor and special recognition instead of purposefully making it part of the church's teaching ministry to the congregation. Perhaps this is part of what Paul cautioned in 1 Corinthians 12:4 – 18, when he describes how the different parts of the body of Christ should be utilized to benefit the whole body. Hands or feet may not necessarily do well as voices!

> A prepared leader, who takes the time to rehearse the passage in advance, can shape the reading's tone, mood, emotion, and sense of flow.

UNLEASH ALL THE BIBLE OFFERS

Thousands of pastors believe that the Bible is God's sacred and inspired Word, but they sacrifice a weekly opportunity to isolate the reading and let that Word speak for itself. I realize that this is often unintentional. Many church leaders have never thought through the subtle message they are conveying to their congregation. Many of these same pastors encourage their people to read the Word personally and devotionally during the week, affirming that the Holy Spirit will illumine it and apply it to their hearts (see John 14:26; 2 Timothy 2:7; 1 John 2:27). But these pastors, if they fail to promote Scripture reading as a separate moment in worship, are missing out on a golden opportunity to model this truth.

I love hearing sermons that unpack the great truths of the Bible, and I look forward to them each week. But I don't know of a single pastor who would want me to rely on the message alone as my only source for understanding the Bible.

Our church's worship director, Tom Jennings, affirms that if readers do their job well, the anticipation of people to hear the message will be raised, even before the sermon begins. "This is why we not only use readers who are skilled, but also ones who understand the theological emphases of the church," he says. Our goal as readers is to give God's Word a platform that unleashes it in all its majesty, power, relevance, and influence.

PART TWO

BUTTERFLIES
*and*BREATHING

CHAPTER FIVE

HOW TO SOUND
LIKE YOU

—✺—

THIS SECOND SECTION OF THE BOOK (chapters 5–8) emphasizes the
mechanics of good reading. You may have skipped the first section (my
personal story), hoping to get to the "meat" and learn how to actually
read the Bible in a way that unleashes its power.

If you struggle with butterflies in your stomach, know that you
are not alone. Even if reading this doesn't completely remove that feeling, I hope you find some helpful guidance in these pages—at least
enough to get your butterflies to fly in formation! For easy reference
on the mechanics of good reading, we have included a short summary
of the ideas included in this chapter in the "Quick-Start Guide" of
chapter 8.

But take caution as you begin! Even if you master all the technical
portions of effective delivery, if you don't personally connect the passage
you're reading to your life, you will miss one of the key emphases of this
book (the heart of the first two sections). As a result, your reading may
lack authenticity. The gap will likely limit your own spiritual progress.
Just as sadly, it may negatively shape the spiritual experience of most
people who hear you.

In Paul's second letter to the Corinthians, he says that God makes
his appeal to the world through "us"—through the personalities, gifts,
and unique voices of people like you and me. God calls Jesus' followers
to be his agents of reconciliation. "And he has committed to us the message of reconciliation. We are therefore Christ's ambassadors, as though
God were making his appeal through us" (2 Corinthians 5:19–20).

God wants to use my lips, my voice, my tone, my pitch, my inflection—and yours too! God wants to make the words of the Bible become living realities for our congregations—through people like us.

The Scripture refers to Jesus as "the Word." Fully God and fully human, Jesus is the eternal, invisible God made visible to us. In Jesus Christ, God becomes a man, taking on human nature and bodily form in what theologians refer to as the incarnation—God "in the flesh." We are told in John 1:1 that "the Word was God," and a few verses later that "the Word became flesh and made his dwelling among us. We have seen his glory, the glory of the One and Only, who came from the Father, full of grace and truth" (John 1:14). Though the incarnation of God in the person of Jesus is a unique, one-time event in human history, we find in Jesus a model for how we can communicate the truth about God. God's written Word becomes "incarnate" by taking on flesh and blood as you and I convey it to others.

> God's written Word becomes "incarnate" by taking on flesh and blood as you and I convey it to others.

The wonder of this divine partnership is just one reason why we need to be in prayer as we begin any reading of the Bible (Figure 1), welcoming God's involvement in every step of our engagement with the text. As you talk to God, tell him your fears and concerns. Affirm that you want to be his instrument. Consider recruiting prayer partners to support you as you prepare to read. You may want to use one of the following passages of Scripture to voice part of your prayer:

- "With God all things are possible" (Matthew 19:26)
- "I can do all things through Christ who strengthens me" (Philippians 4:13 NKJV).
- "Fear not, for I have redeemed you; I have summoned you by name; you are mine" (Isaiah 43:1).

What a privilege it is to use our voices to communicate God's invitation to his people! When we read God's Word aloud, we *become* God's voice to the world. People can expect to hear God's Word through us as we read, and hearing a message from God should be anything but boring, so we must make every effort to communicate that Word with the same passion and emotion that God himself would bring if he were speaking it directly to our listeners. This chapter invites you to read in

Figure 1: Prayer is the first step of preparation.

such a way that you sound like you are having an animated conversation with a good friend.

Is the Real You ... Boring?

For many years my coauthor, Warren, taught a seminary class on worship. He often brought me in as a guest lecturer to teach the students how to unleash God's Word as they were reading aloud during worship services at church—and then how, in turn, to train God's people to do likewise. I usually started my session by modeling what I am trying to teach. One year, I read the story of the apostle Paul casting a spirit from a slave girl, Paul's arrest and beating, his midnight miraculous release from prison, and the instantaneous conversion of the jailor, all stories from Acts 16. Even though I had prepared in advance, I was personally moved afresh as I read it, and so I told it with particular emotion. I'll never forget a comment from one of the students as Warren asked for responses.

"In my tradition, we wouldn't read the Bible like that," he said.

"Like what?" I asked.

"Like it's a story or drama, with so much interpretation and inflection in how you read," he said.

This response puzzled me, because the narrative I selected *is* a story, and is quite dramatic at that. A lot happens in just twenty-five verses!

"How would you read it then?" I probed.

"We'd read it literally, just as it is, straight from the Bible," he replied. I got the sense that he thought I had freewheeled and embellished the Scriptures as I spoke.

"Actually that *was* word for word from the Bible," I explained.

He looked a little surprised and then said, "No, not some special translation — but the one most people use, like in my church our pastor uses the New International Version (NIV)."

"I used the NIV," I said, "and I tried to read it word for word."

I waited because I had hope that he was about to realize something profound — that the Bible could come alive far more powerfully than what he was currently experiencing each week at his church, not because of my gifts or skills, but because the emotional and dramatic power of the Word is there, in the text, just waiting for someone with heart, talent, and appropriate preparation to draw it out.

I had seen this realization happen before with other people I had met. Most people are so used to a lifeless, almost procedural reading of the Bible that they have never imagined that it can come alive with the same level of animation that happens when a script for a radio drama, initially printed on black and white pages, becomes a multisensory, emotion-rich, moving narration at the actual broadcast.

Unfortunately, the "aha" moment didn't come for this seminarian. "Even if you read it word for word, that wouldn't work in our church," he continued. "We want to hear the raw text first, and then the pastor will give us the interpretation."

"What do you mean by the 'raw text'?" I asked.

"Initially we would read it as it's written; you might call it the plain way. Then as part of a sermon, our preacher should be the one to interpret it as led by the Holy Spirit."

I tried to push him just one more time. "What if the reading of the Bible itself *was* the sermon, or maybe the first sermon?" I asked. "And what if the Holy Spirit was just as active in the public reading of Scripture, or perhaps even more so, than in the sermon to follow?" After all, I thought, it's the Word of God, not our human commentaries on that Word, that the Bible says is "living and active" in Hebrews 4:12.

This young man looked puzzled, but I could tell he was curious, so I took that as permission to continue.

"In the earliest days of the church, if the believers in a local congregation got a letter from an apostle, they read it in church as the teaching for that day," I explained, referring to Colossians 4:16; 1 Thessalonians 5:27; and Revelation 1:3. Some believe that Hebrews is a totally intact sermon that was read to various congregations.

"Why can't we take a similar approach to reading God's Word today?" I continued. "The Scripture reader's role would be closely related to the preaching act itself, but it would be limited to the words here in the Bible. When I read, I was in effect taking the words that God has given here and preaching—but not adding to them. The Holy Spirit then uses God's Word to make us eager to hear the second sermon, which is the pastor's explanation and application of the text."

"I still don't think it would work," the seminarian said, dismissing the idea. "If you read it like that, the way people actually talk, then our people won't trust the reading because the reader is making choices about how to interpret it. That should be left to the Holy Spirit."

I didn't continue the conversation further, but I really wanted to!

In one sense, I understand this student's concern. He is genuinely concerned that we don't introduce any unnecessary or harmful interpretation into the reading of the Scriptures. Just give the people the "plain" reading of the Bible, without the dramatic, interpretive "extras," right?

But I see several bigger problems with this way of thinking. I believe that it leads people to think that the Bible is hard to understand and needs to be interpreted *for* them—that they can never engage with the Word themselves. Also, reading the Bible in a flat, detached way does a disservice to it; the practice reinforces negative stereotypes of the Bible as being boring, difficult, and confusing. Even worse, a "plain" read often leads us to misunderstand what the Bible is really saying.

Luke 4:14–30, for example, tells how the village leaders in Jesus' hometown cheer him on by saying they "all spoke well of him" (v. 22). But a minute later they have changed their attitude and are trying to stone Jesus to death. Something has changed. If a reader presents the story in a flat, lifeless way, listeners will be clueless about why the village turned on Jesus. The reader must convey the passion of the unfolding drama so that listeners can fully capture the logic of the story and get an accurate sense of what really happened.

Obstacles to Being Yourself

I'd like to propose a different paradigm for approaching our reading of the text. Make it your goal in reading Scripture aloud that you first try to experience the text for yourself—allowing yourself to enter into the world of the text, meditating upon it, and letting its words really sink into your heart and mind. Once you've experienced it for yourself, you can focus on making it real for others.

I want to give you five models to *avoid* as you seek to read in a way that's authentic, credible, and compelling.

1. Not the entertainer. The focus needs to be on the people or events described in the Bible, not on you as the reader. People can quickly sense if the reader is getting in the way of what is read. At my church, we are sensitive to any reading that is "over the top" and distracts from the text.

Your task as a reader is not to show off your talent. Instead, you want people to hear the Word of the Lord, to capture the meaning through the text as you read. If you let the Bible speak for itself, God's Spirit will engage the imagination of those listening: their dreams, emotions, aspirations, and every other area that can be touched through the spoken word.

2. Not the clown. More than once I've been embarrassed as a reader tried to make the Bible "fun" by starting the reading with a joke or ad-libbing humor to a passage that wasn't intended to be comical. The best way to show the Bible's relevance is to let people see it for what it really is. Don't crack jokes to lighten the mood. Just read the passage.

3. Not a junior pastor. Sometimes, the reader may feel that an explanation, mini-teaching, or a commentary of more than one sentence is necessary before the actual Bible reading. In most cases, this really isn't needed. Nine times out of ten, it is best to go immediately to the passage itself, usually with a simple statement like, "Today's reading comes from Matthew 5:1–12." The congregation rarely, if ever, needs to be told when the text was written or where it was written from. They especially don't need to be told what to listen for as you read. Read the Bible well, and it will whet their appetite for what the pastor, not you, will say next—and it may lead them to do some further Bible study on their own when they go home.

4. Not the unprepared personality. Occasionally, someone will insist that the only "honest" way to read with integrity and authenticity is simply to stand up and start reading with no preparation beyond a prayer. If Boy Scout leaders study their trail map before leading the troop on a hike, are they being any less real? Would a cooking instructor feel that it's inauthentic to study the recipe before leading students through it? Does it lack integrity for a singer to study and rehearse the music prior to leading the congregation in worship?

I hope you see that the obvious answer to these questions is no. In a similar way, it seems inconsistent and shortsighted for people to argue that a reading isn't "real" unless it is done without any thought or effort in advance.

5. Not the bore. When people say, "We don't want the Bible interpreted, we want it read straight," as the seminarian did in my earlier story, I think they're saying, "Be clear but don't try to suggest an attitude or point of view." They're wary of any imposition of the personality of the reader on the text or on those who are listening. They fear that the reader's interpretation will interfere with the work of the Holy Spirit in interpreting God's Word to people's hearts.

I understand their concerns. However, the idea that we can somehow read a passage "straight," presenting it without interpreting it or conveying point of view, is misguided. Intentional neutrality in reading *is* an interpretation. Such so-called objectivity is, in reality, a carefully considered, established, and maintained point of view that says "Hands off! Let's not get too involved with this thing." In an effort to protect the text from erroneous reader interpretations, this point of view chooses to mute the emotional and dramatic power that is inherent in the text itself.[1]

> Intentional neutrality in reading *is* an interpretation.

Making It Real

No bells, no whistles, no smoke, no mirrors — just you and God's Word. How can God work through you so that his Word comes alive in the hearts of people and they experience God through your spoken words?

This section of the book suggests four basic steps, which will be unpacked in the next chapter: (1) break your text down into thoughts; (2) identify the action and flow; (3) let it speak to you personally; and (4) practice your delivery aloud until you feel ready to present it as if you're having an animated conversation with a good friend.

Reading the Bible this way will ensure that you still sound natural, and people will decide that you have something important to say—which is certainly true! God does have something very important to say to the world through your reading of his Word.

A story is told about Mahatma Gandhi, the father of the nation of India, as he studied the teachings of Jesus. Speaking of Jesus and the way his followers treated the Scriptures he said, "You Christians look after a document containing enough dynamite to blow all civilization to pieces, turn the world upside down and bring peace to a battle-torn planet. But you treat it as though it is nothing more than a piece of good literature."[2]

The Word of God is living and active. It doesn't need to be *made* living and active; it just needs to be released—unleashed from the cage that has been placed around it that keeps it safe, boring, and out of date in the eyes of most of the world.

As readers, we need to make sure the living power of God's Word emerges from that cage. Through a good reading of that Word, the Scripture becomes incarnate—taking on flesh and blood and raising the dead to life. God uses his followers to communicate his message to all of creation. Each of us is his witness (Acts 1:8) to make disciples ultimately of the entire world (Matthew 28:19–20). We carry a message of faith that is conveyed by words: "Faith comes from hearing the message, and the message is heard through the word of Christ" (Romans 10:17). Let's learn how to articulate those words so that people can clearly hear and understand what God wants to say to them!

CHAPTER SIX

FROM THE PAGE TO THE STAGE

❦

MY COAUTHOR, WARREN, and his wife, Michelle, went to a concert featuring "The Seven Last Words of Jesus Christ." Composer Franz Joseph Haydn said it took him fifteen years to write the piece, which premiered in 1786 and has been treasured by churches ever since. It is frequently performed toward the end of the season of Lent in many churches.

The music is designed to be a partnership between word and melody. Someone reads a short piece of Scripture as one of Christ's seven last statements, and then the music expresses that particular, dramatic moment during Jesus' crucifixion. The artistic expression lends a sense of intimacy that allows every listener to imagine what it might have been like during the last minutes of our Savior's earthly life.

Unfortunately, that wasn't the experience that Warren and Michelle had at the concert. The orchestra had practiced for weeks, but the reader had obviously not prepared at all. Nor had he considered the setting because he frequently had trouble reading his script in the dim lighting. Even though the passages were fairly short, he stumbled on at least a word or two for most of them.

It was obvious to everyone that he read them unrehearsed, and predictably they had little impact. How much more powerful it would have been if he too had practiced — and if he had considered that he would need a flashlight or pen light!

DEVOTE YOURSELF TO READING THE BIBLE ALOUD

The Bible was spoken before it was written. As the Bible itself declares in describing the process of divine inspiration, prophets, though human, "*spoke* from God as they were carried along by the Holy Spirit" (2 Peter 1:21, emphasis added; see also 2 Timothy 3:14–16).

Paul instructed the young preacher Timothy, "Devote yourself to the public reading of Scripture, to preaching and to teaching" (1 Timothy 4:13). The word "devote" indicates paying careful, heartfelt attention—to study it, work at it, grow, and improve.

That's the opposite attitude of those who say, "I'm not going to make much of this." Sometimes well-intentioned readers, wanting to live out a sense of being natural and authentic, decide not to put any effort into preparation. I think Paul's command requires just the opposite.

> In the early church every service made a special place for the reading of the Scripture.

Bible teachers observe that the verb "devote yourself" is a continuing command. It is to be Timothy's *way of life*. Notice also the word "the" as in "the public reading of Scripture." This is not just any reading. It is "*the* reading." In the early church every service made a special place for the reading of the Scripture. Paul wants Timothy to devote himself to that reading with great care and consideration. "Give your whole attention to it," Paul is saying.

It is also an important *responsibility*. Three responsibilities are stated as parallel: "the public reading, the preaching and the teaching." In other words, the public reading is placed alongside preaching and teaching as something that ministers of the Word should devote their complete attention to.

This is what Jesus modeled in Luke 4:16–21. He read and then he taught from what he read:

> He went to Nazareth, where he had been brought up, and on the Sabbath day he went into the synagogue, as was his custom. And he stood up to read. The scroll of the prophet Isaiah was handed to him. Unrolling it, he found the place where it is written:
>
> "The Spirit of the Lord is on me,
>   because he has anointed me
>   to preach good news to the poor.

He has sent me to proclaim freedom for the prisoners
  and recovery of sight for the blind,
to release the oppressed,
to proclaim the year of the Lord's favor."

Then he rolled up the scroll, gave it back to the attendant and sat down. The eyes of everyone in the synagogue were fastened on him, and he began by saying to them, "Today this scripture is fulfilled in your hearing."

Likewise in Acts we see the church leaders in Jerusalem meeting with Paul and Barnabas to discuss how to evangelize the Gentiles while not being a stumbling block to Jewish concerns about idolatry and sexual practices. Note this comment that emphasizes both preaching and reading: "For Moses has been preached in every city from the earliest times *and is read* in the synagogues on every Sabbath" (Acts 15:21, emphasis added). In fact, the Old Testament describes Moses reading aloud the Book of God's Covenant—and his hearers responding, "We will do everything the LORD has said; we will obey" (Exodus 24:7).

The practice of reading aloud before teaching or explaining the text continued during the time of Nehemiah, where "they read from the

Figure 2: Let the text speak to you personally—this shapes how you will read it aloud.

Book of the Law of God, making it clear and giving the meaning so that the people could understand what was being read" (Nehemiah 8:8). From its earliest years, the church has been committed to separate reading and preaching, as we see both in the New Testament and in early church history (see a second-century quote from Justin Martyr on page 47). It apparently also continues in heaven, as the book of Revelation describes numerous scenes in heaven where various scrolls and books from God are opened and read aloud.

This is why 1 Timothy 4:13 is so vital. Ministers need to give themselves to the reading of the Scripture as well as to preaching and teaching.

So now it's your turn. Here are some steps you can follow as you prepare to go from the page to the stage. Your goal will be to break the passage down into thoughts, identify the action and flow, try to experience the text for yourself, and then practice your delivery aloud until you feel ready to present it as if you're having an animated conversation with a good friend.

Let the Text Speak to You Personally

The first thing you need to do is to let the text speak to you, *personally*. Please don't gloss over this first step. If anything, linger at it. Most of the time when Scripture is being read in public and it lacks a sense of lift, the reason is that the reader failed to prepare. In particular, the reader didn't take thoughtful time to discover the personal meaning that the text has for them. Start your preparation by prayer (see Figure 1, page 62), and then let the text speak to you *personally*—this shapes how you will read it aloud (Figure 2).

While Warren and I worked on writing this book, I was also at work on an adaptation of the great C. S. Lewis classic *Screwtape Letters*, which I then performed in New York City, Washington, D.C., and Chicago.[1] During the preparation, my vocal coach kept saying, "Max, it's still all in your head." That was bad, because she meant I wasn't presenting it with the rest of my being—with my heart and soul as well. It wasn't yet a total body experience, and observers could pick that up. They weren't able to connect with the text and my reading made them feel left out. I was trying to "act" the part of a smart person by voicing academic ideas but not involving myself personally. There was no drama, no "story"—just ideas from a talking head.

When you are preparing and reading the Scripture, you may sometimes feel as if you are talking, speaking the words, but leaving yourself out of the conversation. That's an important sign that you've failed to personally engage with the text. I've got to believe personally in what I am saying and see some type of application to my own spiritual walk. Only then will I be credible and convincing to those I'm talking to. Don't be discouraged if you aren't yet at the point of feeling the text at this level. It is a goal to strive for. If you reach it only partially, the text will still be meaningful to your hearers.

After we actually engage a text, we can build a genuine enthusiasm, a liveliness to our reading because we find that the text is speaking to us. We are engaging in a "conversation" with the Word, and this makes it more interesting and alive for the congregation. If we have a flat experience in our own spiritual processing of the text, that's what we will communicate to our listeners. Blandness comes from an attitude of "I know what this passage says, and there's no need to get underneath it." Blandness also comes from lack of preparation.

How can you get underneath the words to really hear what they are saying? With an open heart to God, read the text very slowly and thoughtfully. Overemphasize the ideas and words. It may even feel a bit unnatural as you meditate on it this way, allowing the text to speak to you. Enter into a dialog with the text.[2]

Let's explore the idea of dialog a bit further. As I have mentioned, the first step in getting to know a text is to establish a dialog with it, inviting it to penetrate and inform your experience. You might want to have paper, journal, or notebook on hand for writing down your impressions. In any case, do not just rely on your memory and think that you can keep it all inside your head. Find some way of writing or recording the ways the text affects you as you begin to read and study it, even if at first you do not receive much from it.

Read the text aloud. At this stage, you are not primarily concerned with oral interpretation. You are simply gathering impressions, sensations, questions, or noting possible problems. Make note of any words that you will have trouble pronouncing or that you do not understand. During and immediately after your early readings of a text you might write out or record your questions for later study.

Remember that you have the Holy Spirit's help. As both the author and interpreter of God's Word, the Holy Spirit can open our hearts to see what God's original intent was for a passage and guide us to apply that meaning to our own situation. One mark of good readers is that they are continually improving their ability to communicate. The word *disciple* literally means "learner," and as disciples of Jesus Christ we should continually be in a learning mode. We approach God's Word as students, asking questions and seeking understanding, before we are ready to communicate it to others.

Block Your Text into Thought Groups

I would encourage you to print out the text you'll be reading (Figure 3). This is helpful so that you can mark it up, but also so you can read it aloud more easily. One of the best websites for finding electronic versions of the Bible is www.biblegateway.com because it provides a dozen English-language versions and more than three dozen other languages, many with more than one translation. It's easy to cut, paste, and print your passage—preferably in a double-spaced format with bold print. As a lower-tech option, you could use a Bible and a photocopier, especially if the machine has an "enlarge" function. With scissors and tape you can quickly create a markable, readable manuscript.

Most people can only receive one thought at a time. For example, you could read the opening verse of the Bible as one thought, "In the beginning God created the heavens and the earth" (Genesis 1:1). But by

Figure 3: Make sure the print is big enough to be readable and that you have enough light to read it.

slowing down, you can focus attention on up to five different thoughts: "In the beginning" "God" "created" "the heavens" "and the earth."

Or consider a passage from Romans. You could breeze your way through a reading of this verse: "Therefore, since we have been justified through faith, we have peace with God through our Lord Jesus Christ" (Romans 5:1).

> Taking the time to break up the text into thought groups is one of the most important steps in the entire process.

Or you could break it into as many as eight separate thoughts for the listener to focus on: "Therefore," "since we" "have been justified" "through faith," "we have peace" "with God" "through our Lord" "Jesus Christ."

My point is not to suggest that you read with long, dramatic pauses, but that you slow down and take the time to discover the richness of what you're reading. Slow down to really listen and focus on the words—this is where the text begins to speak to you. What you receive from the text at this point will be conveyed to your audience as you read. And since people receive one thought at a time, it helps us to "listen" to how the audience will hear the text. Taking the time to break up

Figure 4: Block your text into thought groups.

the text into thought groups is one of the most important steps in the entire process (see Figure 4).

Mark the various thought groups or unique conceptual ideas by using your printout of the verses you'll be reading. Perhaps you could circle various thought groups or put a slash mark ("|") between each one.

A good reading will contain several microscopic (and imperceptible) pauses and inflections that emerge from your study. If you read well, people won't notice what you are doing (your technique), but they will be much more attentive to your reading and will be drawn to notice things that they wouldn't normally see in the text.

IDENTIFY THE ACTION AND FLOW

Adjectives and adverbs help create pictures, but the verbs—the action words—give the speaker energy and power to move the thought forward. As you practice, try giving special emphasis to each verb. Ask yourself: what is the flow of action in this text? What is happening? Am I being asked to do something or respond in a specific way?

Next, outline the text's "emotional" journey. When you read Scripture, you are taking your hearers from point "A" to point "B." This is the journey or the "arc" of the text. It will have a beginning, a middle, and an end. Your preparation will help you discover the emotional flow of the passage. This will give the reading an emotional arc and give the audience a sense that you are taking them somewhere.

> Verbs—the action words—give the speaker energy and power to move the thought forward.

Take a look at this passage from Ephesians as an example: "It was he who gave some to be apostles, some to be prophets, some to be evangelists, and some to be pastors and teachers, to prepare God's people for works of service, so that the body of Christ may be built up until we all reach unity in the faith and in the knowledge of the Son of God and become mature, attaining to the whole measure of the fullness of Christ" (Ephesians 4:11–13). Do you recognize Paul's emotional arc, the journey on which he is taking his listeners? This passage has a clear beginning, middle, and end.

As you break up this passage into its thought groups and meditate on it, the Holy Spirit will begin to speak to you. After rehearsing what you've studied, imagine how you would deliver it to your congregation. It will be quite moving. Think how much would be missed if you merely rattled off this passage as a list without any emotional connection. It would be simply a very long sentence that is unengaged and unengaging. (For a specific example of how I approached a recent reading assignment, including the way I looked for the emotional arc of the passage, see Appendix B, How I Prepare a Scripture Reading.)

Practice with (or Anticipate) a Microphone

If you're reading as part of a family devotional, in a bedtime setting, for small group, or in another setting with only a handful of people, you won't need to use a microphone.

If, however, you are in a setting that offers the option of a microphone, then it's usually best to use it. Ask the person running the sound system about the type of microphone you'll be using. There are many different types of microphones, so if your sound person advises dif-

Figure 5: If using a hand-held microphone, hold it a fist's width (or less) below your chin.

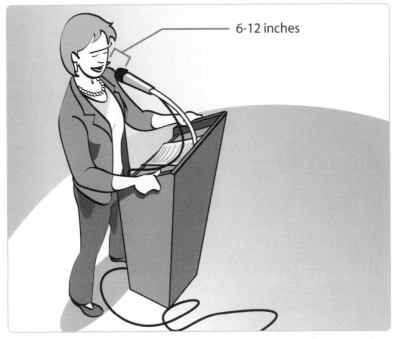

6-12 inches

Figure 6: When using a podium mic, position yourself 6 to 12 inches away, and for a handheld mic clipped to a stand, 3 to 6 inches away.

ferently from what the next paragraph says, go with their instruction. They will typically know what is best for the setting they work with.

Generally, you'll be offered one of three different types of mics. ("Mic" is pronounced *mike* and is shorthand for *microphone*.) Each requires a different distance between your mouth and the microphone's end tip.

Most podium-mounted microphones are designed to work at a distance—between about 6 and 12 inches—whereas handheld mics are often designed to be held a fist's length or less below your chin (Figure 5). As your voice exits your mouth, more of the sound actually goes downward than straight in front of you, which is why the mic needs to be below you, not straight ahead.

When using a podium or lectern mic, position yourself 6 to 12 inches away from it, and for a handheld mic clipped to a stand, 3 to 6 inches away (Figure 6). If you're reading with someone else, then stand as close as is practical to the mic and trust that the sound team will make volume adjustments to compensate.

If it's a lavaliere mic that clips to your clothing (usually on the front of a shirt or dress), make sure your clothing doesn't brush against it.

If you are wearing a headset mic, take the time to adjust the mic so it doesn't rub against any loose hair (Figure 7). If you're a man with a beard, short or long, you'll want to position the tip of the mic so that it is slightly away from your beard.

Please avoid opening lines like "Testing one, two, three," or, "Is this mic working?" Those are unnecessary, add nothing to your reading, and are usually distracting. If you need to test the mic, then tap it gently with your finger or say something very short such as "good morning" or "thank you" (referring to the previous person who spoke). These phrases can be lost without harm to your reading, and they immediately alert the sound team that they need to give volume to your microphone or otherwise activate it.

Prepare for Pronunciation Challenges

Most people appreciate it when their names are pronounced properly. My last name, for example, is not pronounced mac-LEEN but

Figure 7: If it's a lavaliere mic, make sure your clothing doesn't brush against it. If wearing a headset mic, take the time to adjust the mic so it doesn't rub against any loose hair.

mac-LANE. The easiest way to find out how my name is pronounced is to simply ask me or to ask someone who knows me.

When it comes to reading and pronouncing names in the Bible, it's not quite that easy. For starters, we're dealing with several languages (Greek, Hebrew, Aramaic, etc.) and the passage of two or more thousand years. And besides that, do we really want to pronounce the name the way an ancient Hebrew would have said it, or do you want the modern Hebrew pronunciation or the English equivalent?

The same is true with the other biblical languages. When pronouncing people's names, units of measure, or the names of cities, do you want an Americanized English version? If so, you need to decide which Americanized pronunciation you want to use, because many names and places have multiple options that work, much like the different ways people pronounce *potato*.

Here is a basic guide for deciding on the proper pronunciation of a proper noun or word from the Bible:

- Begin by asking whoever will be teaching from this passage how they will be pronouncing the word. "I want to pronounce this word the same way you do. How will you be saying it?"
- Go online and listen to the audio Bibles there, to learn how others pronounce it.
- Consult Bible dictionaries and look for any pronunciation guides.
- Buy a book specifically on Bible pronunciations.
- Use a study Bible that offers pronunciation help.
- If none of these resources are available, take your best guess and then be consistent—don't change the way you pronounce it each time you read.

Most of these resources can be found online. The leading place for Protestants is www.biblegateway.com. For Catholic translations, you can try www.usccb.org/nab.

If you or your church would like to buy a printed pronunciation guide, there are several choices. If you don't mind having a larger volume, go with one of the many Bible dictionaries. These are like short encyclopedias with articles on most Bible-related terms, and they contain a pronunciation guide with each word. These are useful, not only for learning to pronounce a word, but you can also learn a bit more about the person or place when you look it up. One-volume editions include *Nelson's New Illustrated Bible Dictionary: Completely Revised and Updated Edition*[3] and *Unger's Concise Bible Dictionary: With Complete Pronunciation Guide to Bible Names*.[4]

Finally, there are specific pronunciation guides that list every major word in the Bible along with a pronunciation. These include *The HarperCollins Bible Pronunciation Guide*;[5] *Bible Names: Pronunciations and Meanings*;[6] *A Guide to Pronouncing Biblical Names*;[7] *That's Easy for You to Say: A Guide to Pronouncing Bible Names*;[8] and *Lector's Guide to Biblical Pronunciations*.[9]

Just remember the number one rule: whatever you say, say it with confidence. Don't draw unnecessary attention to the word in question. Most of all, don't draw inappropriate attention to yourself. Keep the focus on the passage you are reading, not on your pronunciation of the word.

MATCH YOUR CHURCH'S CULTURE

Much of the way we use our voice is a product of our environment. In the home where I was raised, there wasn't much room for vocal expression. In fact, it was discouraged. Eventually, I figured out for myself how to use my voice in ways that were acceptable for good communication.

Churches, like families, have their own culture. At my church, our Scripture reading team gives serious attention to the feedback we receive from people in our congregation. We're thankful that it's mostly positive. When someone offers negative feedback, more often than not it's because they feel that our readings are "over the top." The worship ethos at my church encourages an even-tempered excellence in communication—not boring, but not overly dramatic either. We have to mediate our desire for animated expression to fit the established ethos of our church.

I'm aware that I have a large and expressive voice. Some people may feel that it's too dramatic. I remember one Sunday when I was reading Paul's speech at Mars Hill (Acts 17:16–34). Afterward, someone in the congregation wrote to tell me that they thought I was being too dramatic. I thought about what they were saying and spent some time wondering if there were other ways to convey Paul's energy and emotion as he presented Jesus to the thought leaders of his day. I realized that in my preparation, I had pictured Paul speaking to a big crowd, so my reading was intended to fit with that image. But what if I had toned it down just a bit, to reflect what it would have been like if Paul were speaking to a smaller, more intimate group without losing his intensity or conviction? That might have worked just as well as the way I had done it. As you can see, it's a continual challenge for readers to faithfully convey the power of a biblical text while matching the culture of their church.

In today's culture, there is also a tremendous resistance to being "sold" — to sounding too much like a salesperson. This is always a danger that interpretive reading might feel too much like a performance and lack authenticity. Despite this danger, the fact remains that people do need to be convinced, and that usually takes energy and passion. I have often used the phrase "You've got to sell that thought" when I'm coaching a reader. What do I mean by that? It means that I'm not getting a sense of passion or conviction from the reading. People look for authenticity, and the best way to sell something today is not through a dramatic performance, but through authentic, personal engagement with the text, as we saw in the previous chapter. Authentic people are "true believers." They are people who believe in their convictions and are passionate about communicating them to others.

> This is always a danger that interpretive reading might feel too much like a performance and lack authenticity.

In many ways, I think the bigger danger to avoid is actually that of underselling. In today's era, people are also afraid to commit, and if I read Scripture in a noncommittal way, it will remain flat on the page. If you have doubts about the best way to read, I would encourage you to err on the side of enthusiasm. In other words, it's better to oversell a reading than to undersell it.

The tone of your voice also affects how well you communicate. I've watched some people try to read with a "voice beautiful" tone: a sonorous, melody-like quality that sounds good but does not communicate. A "voice beautiful" tone will usually draw more attention to the voice of the reader than the message of the text. More importantly, if the reader is not connecting emotionally and intellectually, the reading is not effectively ministering to the people; it ends up being more of a performance.

Practice Until Animation Comes Naturally

Finally, practice your delivery aloud until it comes across as if you are having an animated conversation with a good friend. Your goal is to make public your devotional life with the text—using the words of the Bible and nothing more.

Always keep in mind your listeners. True communication doesn't happen when you speak, but when the content of your communication is received and understood. You have to develop the ear of your listener through your reading. Good listening will give you clues to how you should articulate God's word.

One reason I went into theater was to confront an incredible shyness that was governing my life. I suffered from a stutter, and I was self-conscious. Being prepared is the greatest antidote to a fear of speaking and to avoiding potential stumbles. Even after all these years, I am still working on confronting those fears, but I find it gets better each time I practice well and continue to have the experience of speaking in public.

> Your goal is to make public your devotional life with the text.

As you get on your feet and practice, try to find a place in the church or your home where you can lay out the text in front of you and stand comfortably. It might be helpful to realize that a certain level of nervousness is actually a good sign. Your body is telling you that what you are doing is important and that you need to focus on doing it well. Your goal is to channel that creative energy to work *for* you rather than *against* you. As you become aware of the ways that you twist your hands, shift your weight, or stand too stiffly, you can learn to change those things and practice healthy patterns during your rehearsal. When the time comes for you to present your reading, you will have a practiced, comfortable routine that has prepared you to do your best.

Try to come to the point where you are able to breathe deeply and easily. The next chapter is entirely focused on breathing because proper breathing relaxes much of the tension we feel as we speak.

Let's begin practicing how to read the text aloud.

NOW RELEASE THE PASSION OF THE TEXT

You'll know you've practiced enough when you have a sense of confidence that you know the material well. This means you've gotten to the point where you are able to give minimal thought to the mechanics (where you'll stand, when to breathe, how your text will unfold, etc.).

In many ways, public reading or speaking is just like an important talk you're anticipating with a friend or family member. Hopefully, you take the time to pray about it, rehearse what you want to say, and anticipate different responses; but when the actual conversation comes, you're fully engaged in the moment. You convey the emotions that are flowing

> You should be able to read with the attitude, "I have something exciting and wonderful to tell you."

through you and are fully present in the conversation. With Scripture reading, it's much the same, except that your "conversation" is an accurate word-for-word repetition of the Bible passage.

Or think of it this way. Have you ever taken a lesson in ballroom dancing? If you're still counting or watching your steps, you're not really dancing. In much the same way, people don't want to see the steps you took to prepare the reading; they want to hear the compelling read that is the result of your preparation. They want to see you dance with the text!

You should be able to read with the attitude, "I have something exciting and wonderful to tell you." When the actual moment comes,

Figure 8: Eyeball your *first* line. Now look up and begin your reading.

eyeball your *first* line. Maybe put your finger on the line after that as a place finder. Now look up and begin your reading (Figure 8).

If you've sufficiently engaged the text, you will convey an enthusiasm and a liveliness because the Word has already spoken to you. This experience makes it alive for the congregation. It will be natural as you read to release the passion of the text (Figure 9).

Expression will come as you see the Word of God, visualize it, and try to get someone else to feel it. You don't want people to settle for the low-hanging fruit of the passage — the understanding that anyone can get through a cursory reading of the text. You want them to be able to taste all the wonderful fruit that God has given them through the text at hand. The way you communicate emotion and expression through your reading will elevate their grasp of the text and enable them to pick fruit from the upper branches of the tree.

ANTICIPATE DISTRACTIONS

Distractions are inevitable. So how do you deal with them? Learn to anticipate the fact that there will be distractions as you read. Some

Figure 9: As you read, release the *passion* of the text.

distractions are the kind you can control. I remember one church Sharon and I attended. The reader placed his water bottle front and center at the top of the podium. Our focal point became that water bottle. I elbowed Sharon and teased, "Poland Spring must have given a big gift to their latest campaign." I'll be the first to admit that I drink lots of water, and I often carry a water bottle with me. But when you are reading, try not to make a bigger deal of the water bottle than the Bible.

At another church the typical pattern for the service was to have a large choir sing followed by the Scripture reading. Unfortunately, the reader chose to stand in front of the choir, and the choir was exiting the platform area as they read. The focal point for the congregation was the noise and movement of the choir, far more than the reading. When it was pointed out to the worship director, who was usually on stage and hadn't really noticed a problem, they changed the location so the Bible reading didn't have to compete with the choir.

> If the distraction is really serious, someone in leadership (like the worship director or a pastor) will interrupt you.

Other distractions may be beyond your control. One of the worst church distractions I've experienced happened one Sunday at our church, and I was impressed with how my pastor handled it. A noise suddenly began coming through the sound system. It was a high-pitched buzz that didn't completely drown him out but was certainly distracting. It may have only lasted for a few minutes, but I'm sure the sound team felt as if it went on for several hours. Our pastor knew we were all aware of the noise, but he continued to move forward with the message as if it wasn't there. He was so focused on his goal, preaching the Word, that he wouldn't allow it to divert his attention — and ours.

That said, I've seen the opposite happen as well. A cell phone went off just as a Scripture reader started reading. Understandably, it threw her concentration. Instead of pausing, composing herself and beginning again, she made a comment about how modern technology is annoying. Then she tried to make a joke about it. Meanwhile, time was ticking away, and so was our previous focus on hearing something meaningful from God's Word!

My advice is to just continue going when something like this happens (see Figure 10). If the distraction is really serious, someone in leadership (like the worship director or a pastor) will interrupt you.

Figure 10: If a distraction happens, keep going if at all possible.

Finally, don't let your own reading distract you. Once in a performance of *Screwtape*, I had been struggling with a particular line that on that reading came out quite well—so well, in fact, that I paused to mentally congratulate myself and promptly lost my concentration! Indeed "pride goeth before … a fall" (Proverbs 16:18, KJV). Focusing too much on your own words and how well or poorly you are reading can be a distraction in itself. Your task is far too important to allow anything to pull you off center. You have the words of life, words that people need to hear in order to know how to have right relationship with God, and words that offer help for our brokenness and hope for our eternal futures. You're reading about the Creator of the universe who knows the number of hairs on our head and who cares when a sparrow falls from a tree.

Just as Jesus became human in every way, yet without sin, God's perfect, infallible Word has become accessible to human minds and hearts—and you have the honor of reading it. When the gospel is proclaimed, Jesus is with his people. May that proclamation come through you with passion—and without distractions!

CHAPTER SEVEN

TAKE A BREATH — IT EVEN HELPS WITH NERVOUSNESS

———→·0·←———

POP QUIZ. Imagine that you're at a wedding, and there is someone on stage reading a Bible. What physical clues do you have that let you know that the reader has energy and enthusiasm as they read?

1. Effective hand gestures
2. Animated facial expressions
3. Voice characteristics like volume, tone, speed of reading, and inflection

I hope you chose the third option: the vocal characteristics. The truth is that most people don't. Those who are new at public speaking or nervous at reading gravitate toward hand gestures or facial expressions as their main way of communicating. But that's a mistake.

The best communicators know to put the most study and work into their *voices*, from diaphragm to diction. They give lesser attention to body language, such as hand gestures or even facial expressions. They know that when body language works best, it *follows* what the voice is communicating.

For that reason, I encourage Scripture readers to keep their body relatively still so the spotlight is first of all on their voice, next on their face, and then on their hands. That means that hand pointing and gesturing should be minimal, encouraging more focus on the personality of your voice.

When you overemphasize hand gestures and facial expressions, you drain authority from your message. But when you put your energy in your voice, your authority is enhanced and the words and thoughts you speak are empowered. Take a moment to think about that. Have you ever observed the close relationship between your breath and your thoughts? Your breath is the carrier of your thoughts. Even if someone is standing directly in front of you, you can't communicate very well just your thoughts.

> When you overemphasize hand gestures and facial expressions, you drain authority from your message.

You can try to communicate with your hands and with your facial expressions, but the most important element of good communication will be the words that you use. You need to speak words, and to do that, you need breath to propel them. Having a full voice to read Scripture is essential, and the starting point for having a full voice is your breath, knowing the right way to breathe as you read.

BREATHING AND NERVOUSNESS

We once had a guest speaker at our church for a Saturday seminar. I was sitting in the audience soaking in his talk, and then, unexpectedly, he called upon me to speak. As I began my impromptu response, my voice went dry and my heart started racing. Not being prepared, I felt naked, which triggered all sorts of involuntary responses. I felt a bit embarrassed because I'm used to being prepared. In this case, I made a conscious choice to breathe deeply and slowed myself down. Things began to improve.

Do you know that feeling of emotional insecurity when you are standing in front of a crowd? It is one of the worst feelings in the world! Your voice becomes thin, flat, and high. It has no power. It's almost like being kicked in the stomach. The physical and emotional sense of insecurity is one of the main reasons why public speaking is constantly rated as one of the most frightening experiences for people.

I remember visiting a church where the pastor was preaching about love and was using the Trinity as an illustration. I could tell that he was feeling the pressure of trying to connect to the congregation, but sadly, he was losing our interest. He was feeling intimidated. He wasn't meeting people's expectations, and his failure was getting to him.

As his confidence left him, his voice grew smaller, and it was as if he began to shrink. You could almost see his breath vanishing as he tried to continue with his sermon. His breathing just got shorter and shorter and his voice became thinner and thinner. His vocal reach soon became so limited that the congregation could barely hear him, even though he was still wearing a microphone.

The reason? He simply ran out of air — literally! The emotional connection with the congregation was gone, and he lacked the breath and energy he needed to speak. You could sense that he just wanted to end his sermon and get out of there!

This situation illustrates how emotional factors can inhibit your ability to speak. Keep in mind that they can enhance it just as powerfully. Always remember that the emotions you feel will have a direct effect on your breathing.

This story is not unique. Nor is it limited to those who are relatively new at public speaking. I've seen my own breathing grow short and constricted by feelings of insecurity. Normally, I'm quite comfortable on stage and in front of a crowd, but there are still occasions when I know that I'm not communicating well, and it can begin to affect me. There have been other times when I've received some bad vibes from the audience or felt criticized by them. Sometimes I felt as if the audience was shouting out, "You're boring me." More than once, I've had a reading that made perfect sense as I practiced that simply did not work with the audience. In most of these situations, the problem was more than just my concentration and mental focus. My insecurity affected my emotional well-being, which in turn directly affected my breathing.

> Emotional factors can inhibit your ability to speak.

Our voices are great barometers of our emotional state.

Breathing Calms Your Emotional State

If something unexpected happens as you're reading Scripture aloud and your emotions go haywire, how do you bring your energy and mood back to reading the passage? What you don't want to do is to fake it. Sometimes we try to compensate for this tension by bluffing, by acting more confident than we really are. This pretense of false bravado usually causes more tension.

Instead, stand tall and breathe deeply. This helps you to relax. Relaxation is essential to good speaking. When you are relaxed, the connections between your head and heart, and your breath to your voice, are able to operate unhindered by tension or stress.

> Relaxation is essential to good speaking.

Make full use of your diaphragm, a large dome-shaped muscle that forms the floor of the chest cavity, and don't miss the importance of breathing in communication (Figure 11). Take in more air than you need. When you inhale properly you will be surprised at how much more relaxed and confident you immediately feel. Preferably, do this as subtly as possible without calling attention to what is going on.

If you need to do more to settle your emotional state, then slow down. Slowing down is mostly a matter of self-discipline, like gently

Figure 11: Practice breathing deeply—below your lungs. Make full use of your diaphragm.

touching the brake pedal of your car. Don't screech to an abrupt halt. Simply focus on what you are saying and decrease your rate of speaking.

When I need to calm down, I tell myself words like, "Relax. Don't give in. It will come back." Self-talk like this can really help in a bad situation. You are gaining a sense of perspective and reminding yourself that all you've done is lost your place or stumbled over a word — this is not a national disaster. Your feelings *will* pass, and you will get past the uncomfortable sense of panic or embarrassment that is currently challenging your emotional equilibrium.

> When you inhale properly you will be surprised at how much more relaxed and confident you immediately feel.

We all have horror stories about crises that we've seen or personally experienced in public speaking — perhaps even in the public reading of Scripture. Rarely will you hear a story about how a person recovered from an uncomfortable situation. The reason is that the solution is not quite as dramatic as the problem! The event that throws a person off typically happens in an instant, sort of like a cannonball dive into a swimming pool that suddenly shocks the water. The return to equilibrium, though, is a more gradual process, like the rocking of waves in the swimming pool that slowly and steadily dissipate.

I find it helpful to remember that God has placed his Holy Spirit inside each of his children. And the fruit of the Spirit includes joy, peace, patience, gentleness, and self-control (Galatians 5:22 – 23). As Paul continues in that passage, he encourages us to "keep in step with the Spirit" (Galatians 5:25).

> God invites you to step into his peace and calm as you read.

What does that mean, when we are facing the stress of reading in public? It means that God invites you to step into his peace and calm as you read.

GOOD BREATHING REQUIRES PRACTICE

Taking a deep breath is always a good initial response when you hit a nervous spell as you read, but how do you keep those situations from

Figure 12: Practice aloud at least eight times before your actual presentation.

happening in the first place? Is there anything you can do to reduce the likelihood that you'll panic?

The most important thing you can do to minimize the experience of nervous moments as you read aloud is to practice, practice, practice—and to include "breath practice" in your preparation. The more time you spend going through the various steps we've discussed, the better your chance of avoiding those times when your internal butterflies team up and revolt.

When you are finally ready to work on the mechanics of your presentation, I would encourage you to stand in front of a makeshift podium, take a deep breath, and practice your passage aloud at least eight times (Figure 12).

At some point, while you are practicing, stop and think about your breathing. Power in your speech is driven by your inner convictions, and these will bring passion and life to your reading. Even people with very good voices can still sound disconnected and boring if they are not connected with the text in a personal way. Is the way you're breathing allowing you to access the level of passion you seek? If not, it's helpful to understand a bit about how breath leads to speech.

HOW THE VOICE WORKS

So how does your voice actually work? What happens in your body as you read? Imagine your body as a three-story house. On the top floor are your neck, mouth, nose, and head. On the main floor are your abs, chest, and ribcage. And in your basement is the base of your spine and everything below that — your pelvis, hips, legs, and feet.

Your voice originates when you inhale air (at the top floor) into the lungs (on the main floor). The act of inhaling pushes the rib cage out, relaxing the abdomen muscles around the stomach, and allowing the diaphragm to push downward (into the basement). Most people tend to forget about the basement. If the basement isn't involved — using that dome shaped muscle called the diaphragm (see Figure 11 again) — then you will be short on power when you speak.

The diaphragm is to the voice what the accelerator is to an automobile. Just as the experienced driver of a car knows how to feed gasoline to the engine by pressing down on the accelerator, so too the reader (or speaker or singer) must be able to draw the breath from the lungs and, through correct manipulation of the diaphragm, bring up the necessary stream of air.[1]

Or, to use another image, think of a pyramid-shaped balloon filled with air. The balloon fills your torso, gradually narrowing until it goes through your neck and vocal chords, into your mouth, nose, and head. As you exhale, you should sense the air filling your chest from the base of the pelvis and then traveling up through the throat, vocal chords, and out of your mouth.

When we want to say or read something, our brain transmits a signal down to the pelvic base to release some of the air we have stored. The air is thrust upward with varying force, depending on what you want to say and how you want to say it, through to the top of the "pyramid" into the throat. This thrust of air is called breath. The more force in your breath means more volume and greater intensity. When you are out of breath, you simply cannot speak.

Your breath travels up through your chest and neck and passes your vocal chords. As the air passes through the vocal chords, they vibrate, creating the differing notes of sound we want. Take a moment to put your finger on your voice box at the base of your throat. Inhale and begin to hum. The individual folds of your vocal chord should be producing different notes, much like the different strings on a harp produce different sounds as they are plucked. Hum a higher note and then a lower note to capture the sensation.

Figure 13: Practice taking a deep breath, visualizing your voice in front of you, and letting the air resonate in your lips, nose, and forehead.

These notes are further defined by the resonance produced in your chest, throat, and mouth. The resonance is even affected by the shape of your face, nose, and forehead. The result is a unique audio fingerprint known as our voice.

Does it strike you as odd that I mentioned your face, nose, and forehead as shaping what comes out of your mouth? Speech is the process of breaking up sounds into little units that we call words. All words are uniquely constructed by manipulating our mouth, tongue, lips, teeth, jaw, facial muscles, and the palate at the roof of our mouth. These "articulators" work to produce the huge variety of distinctive ways people express themselves. And all of this happens "behind the scenes"—it's part of the intuitive way we communicate meaning to another person.

But there's more to communication than our tone of voice. For a sound to be heard clearly by someone else in a room, it must leave your body and travel through space. So where you "place" your voice is determined not only by the tone as it is shaped by your body, but by its projectability. In your preparation to read Scripture aloud, practice taking a deep breath and visualize your voice located in front of you. Let the air resonate in your lips, nose, and forehead (see Figure 13) as you direct your voice out and away from your body.

THE ARC OF BREATH

The next step, whether you are using a microphone or not, is to actually project your voice. For best results, you should create an "arc of breath" that originates from the base of the pyramid in the pelvic area. Imagine that you are shooting an arrow into an open field to someone far away. When your voice is launched, it will travel in a rainbow pattern of arcs until it hits the intended target.

Most of us aren't able to create a smooth, clear arc of breath because we are cut off from our full potential. The ideal is that we would have enough breath to propel a thought up through our abs, chest, and throat, and then through the front of our mouth to produce an unobstructed, constant, clear resonance of sound. Too often, we speak from short fragments of breath that begin barely below our chest.

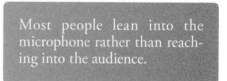

Most people lean into the microphone rather than reaching into the audience.

Our "balloon of air" is small. The arc of breath for good, clear speech requires a deep flow of air.

In my small study at home, I have a simple podium with my Bible on it. When I'm to this point in my preparation, I look out the window and try to imagine that I'm standing in the auditorium of our church. I try to arc my breath toward someone in the rear of the auditorium. I don't yell, and I'm not trying to force my breath out. I simply tap more deeply into that pyramid of air. Typi-

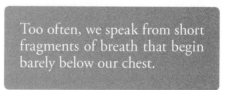

Too often, we speak from short fragments of breath that begin barely below our chest.

cally, this is more effective when I begin by placing my voice on the front of my mouth.

Most people lean into the microphone rather than reaching into the audience. The audience will feel as if they are listening to a private moment, and they will often lose interest. Many people make the arc of

Figure 14: Don't let your voice's arc be too small or too short. Imagine that you're talking with someone in the back of the room.

their voice too small or short. It's best for you to imagine that you are talking with someone in the back of the room (see Figure 14), using a normal, but animated level of expressiveness.

I also see a lot of readers folding their hands or arms as they voice Scripture to the congregation. Symbolically, folded hands represents a closed position. It looks as if these readers are protecting themselves. It also affects the way they breathe, collapsing their breath and pulling in their shoulders so they can't access their pyramid of air. Too often, the readings of people with arms crossed are plain and lack energy, matching their closed stance.

I've had many vocal coaches over the years help me. Some coaching settings have been peer groups, such as when the Scripture readers at our church get together, and for *Screwtape Letters* I hired a professional. In each of these situations, I'm always surprised by how often the concept of *breathing* comes up. Even though I've been reading publicly for many years, a recent coach specifically suggested that I work on improving my breathing—a great reminder to me that this is an area where I can keep improving for the rest of my life.

Good breathing technique is best learned in actual-practice settings, but you may also benefit from some personal reading on the subject as well. In addition to the titles listed in the bibliography, check out your local public library or online sources like Amazon. Simply look under the search word "breathing." While some books on breathing are dry and overly technical for your purposes as a Scripture reader, others are helpful. I just read a book called *Make Your Voice Heard* by Chuck Jones, written at a popular, accessible level.[2] I also recently read *The Breathing Book* by Donna Farhi, which is more technical but gives some helpful advice about breathing correctly.[3]

HOW YOU STAND AFFECTS HOW YOU BREATHE

Did you know that you reveal your age by the position of your spine? The stiffer your spine, the older you look. I first saw this in high school. One of my friends seemed to age fifty years between his junior and senior years. His spine went from being free and flexible to stiff and sensitive. The changes started with the way he walked, but it was soon affecting the way he talked as well. I never asked him what had happened to cause the change, but it had a dramatic impact on his appearance.

When you actually stand at the place where you'll be reading, be sure to keep your feet apart, about even with your shoulders. Keep your knees unlocked (for balance purposes), and let your head float loosely like a bobble-head figure atop your neck (for good spinal alignment), keeping it upright and supported. This posture will help you access the maximum flow of air as you breathe.

BREATHING IS LIFE

Breathing is the first — and last — thing we do in life. The Bible gives us many marvelous images about "breath." We see how God spoke the world into being with "the breath of his mouth" (Psalm 33:6), and the idea of God's breath is a frequent image for the Holy Spirit. The psalmist reminds us that our ability to breath has a purpose — offering praise to God: "Let everything that has breath praise the LORD" (Psalm 150:6).

When communication is at its best, your whole body is united in expressing what you want to say. If you have a clear thought and you're passionate about it, you will find that you have little problem saying

Figure 15: Plan to have a verbally animated conversation with your audience.

what you want to say. Your Scripture reading will be like having an interesting conversation with a good friend. You'll be talking about something that has affected you personally, and you will find that you can convey what you think with genuine, authentic passion, as Figure 15 illustrates.

The more you learn about the art and science of speaking, the more you will learn to appreciate the rich symbolism of God's Spirit as his breath, and you'll grow in your appreciation of the incredible process of creation when "the Lord God formed the man from the dust of the ground and breathed into his nostrils the breath of life, and the man became a living being" (Genesis 2:7).

So take a breath. It does help with nervousness. It also helps your delivery become both more powerful and more natural. And it also reminds you of how the Holy Spirit is at work.

CHAPTER EIGHT

QUICK-START GUIDE TO READING THE BIBLE ALOUD

———⊷◉⊷———

THE MORNING WARREN AND I WORKED on writing this chapter, I had read a passage in my Bible that just wasn't coming alive for me. I knew that if it wasn't personally impacting me, it would probably come across a bit hollow-sounding to anyone listening to me read it.

The passage was from Romans 6:10: "The life he lives, he lives to God." I tried to figure out what Paul was trying to communicate in the verse. I knew that he was talking about Jesus, but in some way these words were also about me: "Now if we died with Christ, we believe that we will also live with him" (6:8). I reflected on what I was reading, but it didn't seem to flow in my mind. It says that Jesus died in order to save others—so is that the reason I die with Jesus, to save other people? No, that can't be right. I'm not supposed to save myself, much less other people.

Then it hit me. This passage is about resurrection. It's a die-to-live emphasis. This section is telling me that I need to see myself as being *already* resurrected with Christ and living out that resurrected life right now within the realm of human possibility. I've been around people who seemed to live like that—much better than I do. They usually strike me as people of great power, but gentle and kind. They seem to have almost unlimited time for me, and they care for me without any regard for what they get in return. They understand that life in the kingdom of God is not just about talking the talk, but about living a life of virtue that pleases God.

I tried applying these insights to my passage to help me draw out the idea of being *alive*. I went back to the phrase that had given me so much trouble with a new emphasis on the idea of living out a resurrection lifestyle: "The life he *lives*, he *lives* to God" (Romans 6:10, emphasis added). That was an "aha" moment for me personally, and I carried that insight into my public reading of that passage.

That's a quick example of how I prepare. I cannot predict that any of my subtext will actually reach the audience. But I know that it affected me. And I have faith that when I allow the Word to penetrate to my own heart, the power of the Holy Spirit will be unleashed in my public reading.

Who knows how God will use it in the lives of those who hear? But I have faith that he does. Whatever text *you* read, my hope and prayer is that it will be unleashed for you, and that you will be freed to share those discoveries as you read to others.

CRASH COURSE — CONDENSED VERSION FOR PREPARING

Suppose you are in charge of selecting the reader for worship. If you do nothing else after reading this book, try to *avoid* the last-minute approach of grabbing someone at the beginning of the worship service or another large-group setting and asking, "Joe, would you read these verses in a few minutes?"

However, if it does happen — and if *you* are the "Joe" who is asked on short notice to read Scripture aloud — here are some things you might want to consider:

1. Ask God to use you as his ambassador to convey his Word to the congregation. Ask him to open up the passage for you. Praying before you read has the added benefit of forcing you to relax and allows God to work through you. Remember that your reading is not about drawing attention to yourself; it's about drawing attention to God and his Word. As the famous first line of the bestselling book *The Purpose Driven Life* reminds us: "It's not about you."[1]

2. Make sure the print is readable. Use a Bible that has a print size that you can comfortably read while standing up. If possible, stand in the location where you'll be reading so you can experience what the lighting level will be and make whatever adjustments are necessary.

3. Find a quiet place to read the passage aloud several times, very slowly and very thoughtfully.

4. Look for phrases or verbs that grab your attention as you read. Allow your voice to express the excitement and energy you are experiencing when you read it.

5. Be authentic and real. When the time comes to actually read, relax yourself by taking a breath. Deliver your reading in a conversational tone, but do it with passion and excitement. Let it come across as if you are talking to someone who is interested in what you have to say. Let your natural enthusiasm come forth uninhibited so that people can see your passion for the passage.

Time on Your Side — Expanded Version for Preparing

Now suppose you have a day or more to prepare. Whether you're about to read Scripture aloud for your first time or your fiftieth time, try following as many of these preparation steps as possible.

Beforehand

1. Pray. Ask God to use this Scripture reading opportunity to fill you with insight and understanding so that you have something meaningful to communicate to others (see Figure 1 on page 62). You can't give to others what you yourself don't have. When I pray, I usually close with the phrase that God will use this reading "for God's glory and our good."

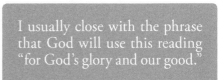

I usually close with the phrase that God will use this reading "for God's glory and our good."

2. Make sure the print is readable. If the print is too small, the lines of type too long, or the print is too faint, enlarge or retype it with a larger type size so that you can read it easily. Or print it out from an online source in large, bold type. You don't want to lose your place or bury your face in the Bible as you read (see Figure 3 on page 73).

3. Understand your text. Good readers demonstrate a deep commitment to an understanding of the text, as if you're trying to receive the mind of Christ. When the text speaks to you personally, it will end up affecting how you read it—which words you emphasize and the warmth or joy that you convey (see Figure 2 on page 70). Good preparation involves a personal commitment to understanding the passage. As the Scripture says, "For out of the overflow of the heart the mouth speaks" (Matthew 12:34; see also Luke 6:35). Let your heart overflow with the truth and power of the passage you are reading.

4. Block out your assigned text. Most people are wired to only receive one thought or unit of information at a time. As you initially read your text (silently or aloud), divide it into natural thought groups. The more complex the thought, the shorter each thought group should be. Next, read each thought block *aloud* slowly, allowing it to speak to you before you move to the next block (see Figure 4 on page 74). For example, John 1:1 has potentially six different thought units: "In the beginning," "was the Word," "and the Word was with God," "and the Word," "was" "God." Breaking up the text into smaller units will open up the text for you in new ways and allow the meaning of the words to penetrate into your mind and heart. If this happens to you personally, it will more likely happen to your audience as well.

5. Find the passion. Your delivery will be the result of preparation and commitment, but the key is to find your passion for the text — that emotional connection to the words. Passion is not something you can manufacture. It's the connection that changes you and gives you the energy you need to communicate with power (see Figure 9 on page 84). When you feel as if you have connected with the mind of Christ in a passage, it propels you forward.

6. Outline the emotional journey. When you read Scripture, you are taking your hearers on an emotional journey. Look for the "story" in your text — a beginning, middle, and end based on your preparation (or look for the peaks, curves, and valleys). This will give the reading an emotional arc and the audience a sense that you're taking them somewhere. Remember that you are partnering with the Holy Spirit to carry your hearers to the right destination — you don't want to miss a turn!

7. Keep practicing. The entire process will involve reading the passage at least *eight* times aloud before your actual presentation (see Figure 12 on page 92). Stand up as you read. You may want to even practice in front of a full-length mirror to make sure your hand motions and other movements are kept to a minimum. As you practice, listen to yourself as if you're the audience. Is what you are saying clear and easy to understand? Are you connecting with the text? Is it speaking to you?

If you practice the passage eight times in a rote, unengaged way, you are following the letter of what we are recommending but not the spirit. If you are actively engaged in the text each time you read it, by the eighth time you will know it so well (and the Scripture will know you) it will be organic and authentic to present publicly. This is the heart of the work. The reading will stand or fall on how well this personal interaction is done.

8. Plan to have a verbally animated conversation with your audience. After you complete your practice and advance preparation, trust that your hard work has served its purpose and relax! (Appendix B shares in more detail an example of how I worked through a text in order to get it ready for public presentation.) Don't try to remember all the mechanics of what you've just done. Put all of your preparation work behind you and simply allow the words to flow out naturally, mostly from your mouth (starting with the diaphragm), *not your hands*. Prepare yourself with the right attitude—you have something exciting and wonderful that you are about to share with your listeners (see Figure 15 on page 98).

> Put all of your preparation work behind you and simply allow the words to flow out naturally

9. Remember the role of faith. Do you believe that God will use his Word as it is spoken through people like you and me? Do you trust that the Word has the power to bring dead hearts back to life? Are you willing to be an ambassador for God? "We are therefore Christ's ambassadors, as though God were making his appeal through us" (2 Corinthians 5:20). Do you share the motivation of the apostle Paul, "For Christ's love compels us" (5:14), as you communicate God's message to others? The ministry of reading Scripture, like any ministry, requires that we depend on God and face any lingering fears with faith. Remember that throughout the Bible God continually commands his people, "Do not fear," as they step out in faith. As you do so, may the words of Nehemiah 8:10 come true for you: May the joy of the Lord be your strength!

10. Rehearse the event. If possible, practice reading the passage in the venue where you will be speaking with the sound system turned on. This is especially important if you are not accustomed to hearing the sound of your own voice being amplified. Practice the entire process: step up to the podium; introduce the text; read it, giving any concluding comment ("This is the Word of the Lord"); make eye contact; and walk away from the podium. For some people, the transitions can be even more awkward than the actual reading itself.

Delivery

1. Position the microphone. Before the actual moment of delivery, try to stand in the exact spot where you are going to read. If there's a hand-held mic, hold it a fist's length below your chin as in Figure 5 (page 76). If you're using a microphone on a stand, place yourself 6 to 12 inches away as in Figure 6 (page 77). If it's a lavaliere mic, your sound technician will probably clip it to your upper body in a way that your clothing doesn't brush against it as in Figure 7 (page 78). Also, if you are wearing a headset mic, take time to put it on well before you need to read so that you have time to readjust your hair if necessary.

2. Take the ready position. Place your Bible or printout in a way that you can see it easily. Stand still, lift your toes to balance yourself, take a deep breath, place your voice forward as if you're about to hum, and imagine that you're throwing your thought out to the congregation through that column of air you're figuratively about to hum. If you need to test your microphone, avoid saying "Testing 1, 2, 3" or "Is this microphone working?" which draws people's attention to all the wrong things. Instead, do it subtly, either by tapping on the microphone, starting very lightly, so that you are almost the only person to know about the test. Or say something short that fits the context of your environment, but would be okay if lost—such as "Good morning" or "Our reading today is . . . ."

3. Speak conversationally but across the room. Imagine that you're talking with someone twenty feet away. If talking could be compared to throwing a football pass, most people's speaking arc is too small and too short (see Figure 14 on page 96). Don't shout, but don't let your voice's arc fall short either.

4. Read with passion. It's time to release the passion of the text (see Figure 9 on page 84). This will happen naturally when you know something well and are convinced of its significance.

5. Slow down by taking deep breaths. If you have a case of nerves, your tendency will be to rush through it. Take bigger breaths than you think you need and pace yourself better. Make full use of your diaphragm and don't miss the importance of breathing in communication (see Figure 11 on page 90).

6. Bookend your reading by looking up. When you start—and also when you finish—the audience will receive your words more readily if your face is not buried in the Bible. A direct look to the audience with a smile always helps. Eyeball your *first* line. Now look up and begin your reading (see Figure 8 on page 83). Look down as you continue into your second verse. The more rehearsed and comfortable you are as a reader, the more you can look up as you read. However, if you must stay glued to the text for the rest of the reading, at the very least, when you're finished, look up and briefly pause.

7. If a distraction happens, keep going. Suppose a cell phone rings, a baby wails, or a door closes noisily. These temporary diversions are part of life. You have a life-giving message to share that is far more important and engaging than a momentary interruption. If you stay on task and focus, almost all your hearers will follow you. In fact, if you continue in confidence, you will show that the distraction does not bother you. Therefore it should not bother them. It helps everyone to move on (see Figure 10 on page 86). If the distraction is really serious, someone in leadership will intervene, so you should keep going unless someone asks you to pause.

Part Three

HOW
to TEACH
OTHERS

———◆———

CHAPTER 9

TRAIN YOUR PASTOR TO READ THE BIBLE BETTER—REALLY!

⟨⟩

I KNOW OF A CHURCH where the senior pastor has dyslexia, a medical condition that causes his brain to play tricks on him when he's reading. This pastor memorizes his sermons, and his delivery is passionate, powerful, and articulate—with no noticeable negative impact from his dyslexia. He has such a reputation as an effective communicator and capable leader that most people would never guess that he has a learning disability.

When he reads something aloud as part of a sermon, however, it's a night-and-day contrast. Whether he's reading a Bible passage, an email he received, a quote from a book, or anything else in printed format, his dyslexia kicks in and his fluid speaking style collapses. Even if he practices in advance, he inevitably stumbles, transposes words, or slows to a crawl. Listening to him at that point can be downright painful, and people's attention shifts from his content to his person. "What's happening here?" people ask themselves since most of his church is unaware of his condition.

The church's worship leader, administrative assistant, and associate pastor—as ministry colleagues whom he trusts—have each spoken privately with him about the situation, exploring different alternatives. One of the recurring suggestions they make is to use someone else to read any lengthy writing that he'll be using, whether it's the Bible or a sermon illustration. The conversation tends to go something like this:

"My reading is not that bad."

"Yes it is," his staff will reply.

"Well, it's too much of a pain for us to line up readers."

"But it's more of a pain to listen to you read!"

"The switch between me and another reader would distract the congregation," he'll say.

"You don't know that."

Some of the church's elders have also initiated similar conversations with the pastor, although they were a bit more gracious and less blunt.

After several years of these back-and-forth dialogs, the pastor finally decided to give it a try. The first step was for the worship leader to ask gifted members from within the congregation to read the main Scripture passage before the pastor's teaching began. The first recruits were a schoolteacher, a nurse, and a salesperson. All were highly involved in the church and had obvious gifts as storytellers. That worked well, and the congregation responded positively to the change, with many commenting that they appreciated the extra attention given to the Bible by making the reading into a separate event.

A year or so later, the pastor agreed to take another step: having a reader handle any long readings that occurred during his teaching, such as times when there was a lengthy in-message Bible passage, a letter he had received, or an extended quote.

By this time, he and his readers had already developed a cue system, so the reader knew exactly when to rise from a front-row pew and climb the front steps to the podium. This, along with a handheld microphone for the readers, made the transitions almost seamless. The pastor continued to handle short lines by himself, but the readers did all of the longer reads, which would typically happen every few weeks. The church had more than one service, so there was a different reader for each service (someone who regularly attended that service), for the times when the pastor wanted help.

For Pastors and Teachers

If you are reading this and are a teaching pastor at your church, I realize that you may not have dyslexia. You may have never heard anyone comment negatively on the way you read Scripture as part of your message. You may even commonly embed the Scripture reading within your message in such a way that it would be difficult to isolate it as a separate event. Like many pastors, you may follow a common pattern where you begin your message with a story or a description of a problem. Then, after engaging the congregation about an issue or need, you begin reading from the Bible, sometimes reading just one portion at a time with instruction, application, or exhortation in between each verse or phrase.

If that describes you (or your pastor), would you try an experiment by adjusting your style so that the reading of Scripture becomes more isolated and prominent? Personally, I recommend to pastors that they consider the equivalent of reading the passage twice — once prior to the teaching and again within the sermon, as a way of reinforcing the passage.

> Most people actually need to hear the Scripture twice to really hear it and understand what it is saying.

Most people actually need to hear the Scripture twice to really hear it and understand what it is saying.

You may have spent the entire week thinking about the passage, reading and reflecting on it all, but for most people, this is their first exposure to those words. The first time the audience hears it, they're just becoming familiar with the general direction of the author's thought or the plot of the narrative. They are just beginning to discover some level of the author's intent. The second time the passage is read, during the message, the congregation can take time to focus on the details and start grasping the points the pastor wants to bring out through the message.

For that reason, whenever I am leading a Bible study I make it a regular practice to make sure that the passage is read twice. So I don't believe there is any contradiction or duplication if you isolate the Scripture before the message and then reread portions or all of it as part of your sermon delivery. With a slight alteration from the pattern of preaching described earlier, it is actually easy to introduce an isolated Scripture reading, give an introductory story and overview of the message, and then reread the passage, either as a whole or portion by portion.

For Trusted Lay Leaders

Suppose you're reading this chapter and you're not a member of the pastoral staff, nor do you have a major volunteer role in worship. Yet you'd like to see a greater emphasis on the public reading of Scripture in worship. What can you do?

Let me encourage you to begin by seeking God's will in prayer as you prudently and patiently look for opportunities to discuss this with your church's leadership. A note or comment written in a positive, constructive spirit is almost always well received by the church staff. You'd be surprised how often they receive communications that are harsh in tone. Next, try to figure out what feedback loops are already in place as the most natural channel for this discussion. Maybe there's an elder board, a worship design team, or another structure that focuses on this issue. If so, it's best to start there.

Also, look to see if there are people who already have an inside track with the teaching team at your church. Is there someone in the congregation whom they respect and look to for advice and feedback? If so, maybe it's good to start with that person, but only if done appropriately. This is not to be a pretext for criticism or manipulation.

Whomever you speak with, you want to avoid anything that comes across as disrespectful, disloyal, adversarial, or divisive. It's always a good idea to do your next step one-on-one, rather than in a public setting.

Suggestion

Take the approach of offering a suggestion. Avoid any tone of being insistent. Be humble and caring. Ask permission to introduce your subject, such as "May I offer a suggestion for you to consider?"

Experiment

In your suggestion, ask if the pastor (or worship design team, or elder, or whoever) would consider an experiment. Remember that most churches — and people — change incrementally, one small step at a time. Perhaps use a phrase like, "Do you think we could test the water with something?"

Agreement

Make your point in a way that appeals to something your church's leadership already agrees with. Approach the subject in a way that you're speaking to a value that the church already supports, and your improvement might simply help it be expressed in a better way. Use the word *and* more than *but*. For example, "One of the many things I love about this church and your ministry in particular is the importance we place here on God's Word, the Bible, *and* so I was wondering...."

Big Picture

Briefly describe the "what" and the "why." Here is how I communicated to our worship leader after Sharon and I committed to joining the church we had been attending for about eighteen months, after going through the six-week membership process, and as a final step publicly confessed our vows to this local body of Christ at a morning worship service.

> Dear Tom:
>
> Thank you for allowing me to introduce myself yesterday prior to the 6:00 p.m. service. I am a new member of Redeemer. My wife and I made our membership vows in January. As a new member I've been thinking about how I might make a contribution to our church.
>
> I am trained as an actor. For the last 17 years my work has concentrated on the oral interpretation of the Bible....
>
> The area that I believe I could be of specific help at Redeemer is to encourage actors and gifted speakers to draw compelling moments out of readings of the Bible in public worship. Initially, I would like to help people catch the vision of what could be done. The longer view is to audition, enlist, and teach a committed group of actors/readers to "devote yourself to the public reading of Scripture" (1 Timothy 4:13) at a high level whenever it is requested....
>
> Sincerely,
> Max McLean

Depending on how you tailor your approach to the appropriate leaders at your own church, you might then conclude by saying, "So I was wondering if we might explore an idea that would involve gifted speakers to draw compelling moments out of readings of the Bible in our public worship."

Word Choice

For most people, the word *change* implies loss. In making a change, not only will they lose something, but they'll also need to make some form of emotional transition — and adjusting to a change is often harder than the change itself. So if possible, avoid using the word *change*. Instead talk about strengthening, improving, developing, expanding, enhancing, enriching, tweaking, sharpening, brightening, focusing, or going to a new level. For instance, "By involving skilled and committed laypeople to read Scripture, it might take us up another notch in the congregation's engagement with the Word."

Timing

Think of a natural time when the change might be introduced. If it's the fall season and your church does something special for each week of Advent, you could suggest starting the readings then. If it's January, and your church does a marriage renewal emphasis near Valentine's Day, suggest that engaged couples—ones with appropriate skills and commitment—do the readings each weekend in February. If your church does a youth Sunday service, then propose a month surrounding it with the youth group's most capable readers. If your church has a prayer emphasis week each fall for the kick-off of the school year, propose that those educators in the congregation with strong presentational abilities might be the readers across August or September. Whatever your context, be ready with an idea or two of *when* it might happen. "Maybe, for example, we could kick off this experiment in Scripture reading by …." (The concluding chapters of this book have further advice on how to enhance the existing culture of Scripture reading in your church.)

> Avoid using the word *change*. Instead talk about strengthening, improving, developing, expanding, enhancing, enriching, tweaking, sharpening, brightening, focusing, or going to a new level.

For Pastoral Staff Members

If your role is similar to the associate pastor listed in the opening story of this chapter, then it's appropriate for you to initiate a conversation. One way to do so in a positive tone is to ask each week any of the following questions that would best match the environment and theology of your church:

> Do any parts of the service need special attention before next week?
> What's your sense of how things flowed together in the service?
> Where did God show up most visibly in our service?
> Where in our worship services this weekend do you think God's blessing was most evident?

Any of these questions in themselves usually invite an excellent exercise for learning and growth. At some point the discussion will likely come to the role of Scripture, and you can use the sequence suggested above to explore ways to further elevate the experience of Scripture reading.

You could also bring up the findings from the Reveal study (see chapter 2), which is leading many churches to place a greater emphasis on the public reading of Scripture—done well—as a way of helping people do better application in their personal spiritual journeys.

YOUR PASTOR'S EAR

Leaders of volunteer organizations, and especially churches, tend to receive a lot of feedback from members who care deeply about what's going on. In any given week your pastor probably receives negative reactions or awkward suggestions from more people than you might imagine! This happens in every kind of church, from declining congregations to thriving ones. Some people whine, some criticize, some are angry, some are frustrated, some are downright mean, and some are simply confused.

Whatever the case, you need to be keenly sensitive to the fact that any modification of the worship culture at your church will involve a relational cost. It can lead to emails, letters, phone calls, hallway conversations, or other formats in which something lands on your pastor's desk. It will require time, care, and prayer in response.

In preparing to write this book, Warren and I asked lots of people, "Please tell me how Scripture reading is done at your church." In one instance, a long-term church member replied, "I don't like the way they changed the Bible translation." After hearing her out on that issue, we asked the question again. "We have a new reader and she usually wears a robe and a hat." We still weren't getting to our question, so after listening further, we asked yet again. "Our new pastor does it differently from our old pastor." We were getting closer, but it took quite awhile to finally talk about the reading itself.

> If you disrupt the culture too much, the disruption is all that will be seen — not the better reading of the Bible.

Our interview reminded us that each church service has its own culture. We were reminded that if you disrupt the culture too much, the disruption is all that will be seen—not the better reading of the Bible.

It's vital to introduce an elevated reading of Scripture within the culture of your church. At Redeemer Presbyterian Church, our worship cadence is one of simplicity, and we try to avoid unnecessary flair. So when our reading team began doing weekly Scripture readings, we tried to stay with a style of dress that was casual but appropriate. We weren't part of the pastoral team who wear coats and ties for morning worship (they are more casual for the evening services), and we weren't simply a part of the congregation, where dress can range from Sunday best to shorts and a tee shirt. So we tried to find a happy medium, knowing that it will be noticed negatively by some if we are too casual. We've also observed that it is usually appreciated if we veer toward the more conservative coat and tie for men or business attire for women.

Since our morning services are more formal, we have found that it is not appropriate for us to have any prereading banter, with the possible exception of a brief "Good morning." Our practice is simply to begin with, "The Scripture reading is from ...", take a breath, and begin. We use the same Bible translation as the teaching team, and we stay with the same level of formality in tone. We are especially careful not to go "over the top" in how we read, since that would be too jarring for the culture at Redeemer. I am sometimes accused of being "too dramatic," due primarily to the size of my voice and the nature of my work in the theater. Such comments remind me that occasional criticism is probably unavoidable for anyone in leadership.

> The most important thing you can do is to recognize the culture of your congregation and match the Scripture reading style accordingly.

Within these standards, we sense a great freedom of range in how to make the Bible come alive — and it does! We also listen carefully to any comments from the worship director and pastors. Even so, the staff does receive congregational comments on our reading, and it passes them along to us. We take them seriously and are constantly stretching ourselves to fit better within the culture of our particular church.

Your church may be totally different, and I'm not inviting you to become like my church in its level of formality. Instead I want to emphasize that the most important thing you can do is to recognize the culture of your congregation and match the Scripture reading style accordingly.

Start with Seminary and Bible College

What about seminaries, Bible colleges, and other places that train future pastors? My coauthor Warren Bird has taught at Alliance Theological Seminary since 1985. In courses like "Worship" and "Communication," he's added Scripture reading to the course material, sometimes bringing me in as guest lecturer. What surprises him most is that no student has ever said, "I already do that" or "that's what our church always does." Instead, the idea of selecting talented and spiritually committed readers, asking them to practice the passage many times in advance, and improving the quality and impact of Bible reading is consistently a new idea. It's typically well received, but it always appears to be novel.

One of America's best trainers in preaching is Haddon Robinson, Distinguished Professor of Preaching at Gordon-Conwell Theological Seminary. On three occasions he has invited me in for a day-long seminar to work with his doctoral students. What stuck out most to me is that these very able students, who understood the passage, had read and studied it, and knew how to bring out theological and practical applications to the text, had such a hard time reading it aloud.

Until those experiences, my working thesis had been that a thorough understanding of a Scripture passage would translate into an informed, connected reading. After all, a good reading is merely a connection between clear thought and vivid speech. Many of these students were lively preachers and storytellers.

But when it came to reading the Scripture passage on which their teaching was based, their natural desire to communicate was lost. It was almost as if they had all listened to a tape somewhere that had taught them that "Scripture must be read in a flat and bland way so as to hide its full intent. Meaning will emerge only after I explain it to the congregation."

One student had selected Psalm 137, a psalm that ends with the abrupt and emotionally charged statement, "Happy are those who seize your infants and dash them against the rocks" (TNIV). Why he selected it, I don't really know, but when he was called to read it in front of the class, he delivered it as if that powerful and perplexing climactic line wasn't even there. If you are going to read that text, you certainly can't bury that verse! I read the nine-verse psalm several times to him, asking him each time, "Do you see it? Are you aware of it?" Eventually, the lights clicked on, "Oh, I see it now."

I suspect Haddon Robinson would never allow anyone to select such a controversial text without exploring the reason for its unusual, unsettling conclusion. In today's culture, a statement like that becomes an immediate elephant in the room. Yet by his reading, the student was allowing that elephant to roam wildly, pretending that it wasn't even there! While this might be an extreme example, it unfortunately represents a pattern I have seen far too many times.

Most of the books on the topic of reading Scripture aloud come from the pen of seminary professors. They address a wide range of topics, from how to read different parts of the Bible (poetry, narratives, etc.) to how to interpret the passage you'll be reading (by use of Bible commentaries, Bible dictionaries, etc.). There are only a handful of such books in print, and many of them are listed in the bibliography of this book as helpful tools for you.

> Why don't more churches want Scripture reading to be one of the high points in the worship service?

But none of these books asks the question, "Why don't more churches want Scripture reading to be one of the high points in the worship service?" Nor do they squarely address the follow up question, "How can our church move from where it is now to a place where Bible reading is elevated and receives just as much preparation as the music?"

I believe that the core issue is the one illustrated in the opening barber shop story of this book: for many people, whether at seminary or in pulpits, these are simply ideas they've never thought about. Perhaps it's because they've never really seen a good model.

National Shift

The tide may be turning as we see a growing emphasis on a heightened role of skillful Scripture readings in worship. As churches reach out to those involved with the arts, more actors, artists, and vocal professionals are being drawn to the gospel of Jesus Christ and are bringing their gifts into the service of the church. Church leaders want to empower God's people to serve, and there is a growing awareness that certain models of worship have inherent limitations that downplay the Bible and the focus of historic Christian liturgy.

CHAPTER TEN

INVITE YOUTH AND CHILDREN TO MAKE SCRIPTURE COME ALIVE

HAVE YOU EVER HEARD SOMEONE SAY, "I'd rather die than speak before a group"? Well, they may not be alone! In a ranked list of what people fear, notice that speaking in front of a group is the number one fear, way *ahead* of dying!

1. Fear of speaking before a group
2. Fear of heights
3. Fear of insects and bugs
4. Fear of financial problems
5. Fear of deep water
6. Fear of sickness
7. Fear of death[1]

Many of our fears grow out of a sense of inadequacy or a fear of what other people think about us. And that can be particularly true for children and youth, when asked to read aloud in front of their peers or adults. While some children are bold and fearless when asked to speak in front of others, others are terribly self-conscious. But fears like this don't need to keep them away from reading the Bible aloud with both heart and meaning.

A Surprise in the Christmas Service

I remember the year my church—the same one in New Jersey where I did my first Scripture readings—put on a "Glory of Christmas" production for Christmas. I was responsible for producing the entire event. All of the various children's Sunday school classes were assigned to do a part in the program, and it felt a little like herding cats—chaotic and disorganized with kids going every different direction.

The day of our big production finally arrived, and the sanctuary was packed with parents and relatives of the children, plus a few neighbors who had been invited. The program, as expected, was filled with the chaos of traffic jams on the stage. At one point, though, a sweet and confident seven-year-old girl rose to do her part in the program, a reading of the Christmas story from Luke 2. This is not an easy story to read. It begins with the announcement of a taxation decree from Caesar Augustus (which is not an easy name to rattle off), and then adds the further challenge of saying that this happened "while Quirinius was governor of Syria" (vv. 1–2). It goes on to describe the birth of Jesus, shepherds who were "terrified" by an angel (v. 9) and who "hurried off" (v. 16) to find the baby, people who were "amazed" (v. 18) as they heard about the miracles of that night, and how everyone was "glorifying and praising God" (v. 20) for all the things he had done.

This tiny little reader read through the passage with empathy and passion. She didn't stumble over a single phrase (not even over the name Quirinius). Her reading really shined that night. She had put a spotlight on the story of Jesus and his birth, making it the most important event of the evening.

When she finished reading, the entire congregation was silent. I was the host for the evening, so I paused and let the moment hold for just a second. Then I heard myself say to the young reader, "That was a *good* read!" The audience laughed heartily at my understatement. There was a sense of joy at how good it really was, and then they applauded.

Children Can Make Scripture Come Alive

When a child reads well, people listen. This girl's innocent-sounding, credible, high-pitched voice gave a fresh sense of power and truth to an oft-heard biblical account. It warmed our hearts and for some may have strengthened their faith.

How was she able to read it in that way? Clearly, this wasn't the first time she had read the text. Had that been the case, her voice would have almost certainly been lost in that cacophony of songs, sayings, scenery, and children tripping as they ascended and descended the stage.

When I first met this young girl, I could tell that she had a heart for God and was a strong reader. I rehearsed the passage with her, as her parents watched, and I'm certain they continued practicing at home. I had read Scripture several times at that church, so they were familiar with the way I read and knew how important it was to me that their daughter carefully rehearsed the reading. We had also practiced where she would stand, position her script, and use the microphone.

That evening, their daughter was so well prepared that she appeared comfortable standing in front of an audience of adults. Her reading was expressed in a way that sounded both organic and intuitive for the audience, the result of her natural skill and hours of practice with the Scripture passage. You could also tell that she loved the game (so to speak) — it was a joyous experience for her, and her joy overflowed to us. That's why the audience laughed. Above all else, I think her role as reader conveyed an important message that evening, that kids are important to God and to church, and that there's room for them to play an important role in worship.

> The seven-year-old girl's role as reader conveyed an important message that evening, that kids are important to God and to church.

MODELING IS VERY IMPORTANT FOR CHILDREN

The numerous experts in children and youth that we consulted for this chapter, who were the source for most of the advice in this chapter (and are named in the acknowledgments section), all affirmed the important role that Scripture reading can have on children and youth. One of the themes they emphasized most is the role of modeling, starting with early childhood.

Most young readers have not yet mastered the skill of interacting with text. Children are still learning what it means to have a running conversation with the text in their heads. When teachers model that skill for them, it's called "thinking aloud." Children need to observe and experience what it's like for a mature reader to *interact* with the Scripture while reading rather than merely recite the words. Most will not be able to do this on their own without a lot of guidance. For children to learn to read Scripture well, it is important that they see and experience good models of engagement with the biblical text.

> Children are still learning what it means to have a running conversation with the text in their heads.

It's best for children to begin by reading a passage they can understand. They are concrete thinkers, so avoid a passage full of symbols and complex logic. If the passage contains an abstract idea, it should be carefully explained to the child so he or she can read it meaningfully rather than sounding stiff and wooden.

When I read for children, I've found that I am able to draw their undivided attention by reading a relatively short story. This is especially true if I am able to tap into the natural power of a story to engage their hearts and emotions. I once remember reading from the Gospels about the lame man whose friends lowered him through the roof so that Jesus could heal him (Mark 2:1–5). As I read, I could tell that the children were engaging with the story in their imagination, visually picturing the events in their head and soaking up the images and feelings that the story creates for the listener. It doesn't matter if we are adults or children; when we see ourselves in the story and are able to engage it with our imagination, we will have greater opportunity to apply it to our life.

As you model how you interact with the text to children and youth, think of ways to make the biblical text as accessible as possible to them. Children typically learn best when they experience something in a variety of different ways that engage the senses. By acting out the story, for example, they will attach a visual and/or kinesthetic facet to the reading. These types of associations help them experience the text on a deeper level.

Likewise, children-friendly Bible translations can make the text more accessible to their level of understanding. Several different children's versions exist, plus a host of illustrated Bible storybooks that cover a variety of different maturity levels. As an example, you could use a book like Ella K. Lindvall's *Read-Aloud Bible Stories* (see Bibliography) with preschool age, early readers to help them engage with the Scriptures at an appropriate level. Just like language groups around the world need a translation that speaks their heart language, children need exposure to Scripture that speaks at their level of understanding. We are so fortunate in this country to have a wealth of resources for children—but they're helpful only if we use them!

This is not to say that young people should never read from or be exposed to adult versions, but we should try to give children the experience of reading Scripture for themselves as soon as possible. Children's Bibles are a great resource for doing this. If you do use an adult-level Bible translation with children, remember that it is probably above their reading level. They need to have adult support or they will become frustrated with the text. Be sure to explain the difficult words or unfamiliar phrases in a way they can understand.

Finally, as you model good skills of oral reading for children, remember to model the mechanics as well. Children will need to rehearse all the details of reading in a public setting, such as walking onto and off of the platform, using a microphone, speaking slowly and distinctly, and perhaps anticipating an interruption, such as a baby crying or a noisy fire engine passing by.

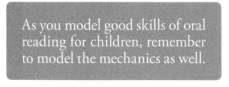

As you model good skills of oral reading for children, remember to model the mechanics as well.

As you rehearse each aspect of reading with them, consider involving their parents or other relatives. I have one friend who, when serving as volunteer Christian education director at a small church, would meet with the family on Saturday for rehearsal. He would explain how important it is to read God's Word as a way of helping the family learn to take it seriously. When the children saw their parents' positive attitude and commitment, they followed their parents' lead.

All of the preparation paid off on Sunday morning, as the children's readings were meaningful to the congregation, not just something "cute" for the kids to do. As people expressed gratitude and thanks to the family, it helped create a church culture that elevated Scripture reading for members of all ages. When the children ask their parents, "Can we do this again?" you know something good is happening at your church!

If you are a parent (or aunt or neighbor to children), it is also important that you not underestimate the impact of reading the Bible aloud at home, as we discuss in more detail in the next chapter. In our home,

Sharon and I consistently read the Bible to our two daughters. Sometimes they'd even play church, talking fast gibberish from a play pulpit and then slowing down occasionally to say "baby Jesus" as the punch line.

But our Bible readings really did have an impact on them! I remember one day our daughters were playing with two other girls, and one of them was mean to our younger daughter. Rachel, our older, wanted to confront the mean treatment, so she ran inside the house and asked pointedly, "Where's my Bible? I need to show them that verse, 'be kind ... to one another'" (Ephesians 4:32). Then she ran back out and showed her playmates the verse. It was fun to see all the girls looking at the verse, talking about it, and then changing their behavior to fit the teaching of the Bible. That's really what this is all about, isn't it? When kids read the Bible, the Word is planted in their heart in ways that can lead to lasting changes for years to come.

YOUTH TOO CAN TAKE THE BIBLE TO HEART

Many of you reading this book have probably attended the music recital of a child or young person. You may have noticed that not all performances are the same. While some students simply learn how to play the right keys in the right order, others have taken their playing to the next level—they have figured out how to interpret the song and play it with expression.

Just as a good piano recital is more than merely hitting the notes, Scripture reading involves more than reading words on a page. If the only thing the student knows is how to play the "notes" or "chords" of the piece they are reading, the music comes across as clangy, awkward, and even boring. Often, we end up focusing far more on the musician and how the musician might be feeling than on the music being produced.

The same is true when it comes to reading Scripture, and no one senses the contrast between a good reading and a poor one more than youth. They often lack confidence and are extremely self-conscious when they make mistakes. They can be embarrassed by their poor reading skills, and often it takes just one public mistake while reading for them to shut down, to avoid being laughed at by their peers.

My coauthor, Warren, recently told me about his experience watching a handful of youth who were involved in a Bible quiz team. They had each memorized a dozen or so chapters of the Bible with incredible accuracy. The youth teams competed with each other to be the first to state a verse from memory when the quiz master announced its chapter and verse number. What struck Warren as unusual was how they quoted the Bible with such care, thoughtfulness, and even passion. When called upon, they didn't just rattle off the words of Scripture that they had crammed into their heads. As they practiced mastering the verse from memory, they must have been thinking about the meaning of the verse as well, because when the words came out they reflected genuine engagement with the text.

Something for Everyone to Do

Here are five creative ideas suggested by some friends in youth ministry that can help youth and children learn to practice reading Scripture aloud. Perhaps some of them will work for your context!

1. Present the Scripture as a Team Effort

You may designate and coach one or two people as the actual readers, while the rest can play other roles. Perhaps one of the nonreaders can design the way the Scripture will look on the overhead projection or in the printed bulletin. Another can check and adjust the microphone or even run the sound board. Another can be responsible for makeup and props, if needed. Another can videorecord it. Be careful, though, not to demoralize youth by roles that affront them as patronizing or busy work.

2. Take a Reader's Theater Approach

Some group reading approaches can be done quite simply, such as one person reading the love chapter (1 Corinthians 13) and the youth group saying the word "love" each time it appears. Other group reading approaches are more complex and require careful rehearsal to be delivered effectively, such as the prophet Nathan's rebuke to King David, which led to his repentance in 2 Samuel 12:1–22. Readers might involve one or two narrators and designated readers to portray the voices of David, Nathan, the Lord, and David's servants.

3. Mime a Passage as Someone Else Reads

We have seen visually compelling enrichments of Scripture reading by choreographed and rehearsed pantomiming that accompanies someone's skillful reading. Many passages are so image-rich that they almost beg for artistic expression. Imagine what a youth group might do in developing a mime pattern for the following passage from Psalm 42:1–6.

> As the deer pants for streams of water,
>   so my soul pants for you, O God.
> My soul thirsts for God, for the living God.
>   When can I go and meet with God?
> My tears have been my food
>   day and night,
> while men say to me all day long,
>   "Where is your God?"
> These things I remember
>   as I pour out my soul:
> how I used to go with the multitude,
>   leading the procession to the house of God,
> with shouts of joy and thanksgiving
>   among the festive throng.
>
> Why are you downcast, O my soul?
>   Why so disturbed within me?
> Put your hope in God,
>   for I will yet praise him,
>   my Savior and my God.

4. Create a Background Video or Painting As Someone Else Reads

Like the previous idea, a similar approach can be taken using other arts, such as crafting a painting as someone reads Scripture or preparing a collage of video images to accompany selections from Scripture. Suppose someone were to read selections from John 6:1–40 on Jesus as the bread of life. Any number of artistic expressions could bring out the richness of these concepts as someone reads them aloud.

5. Use Creative Curriculums

There is a large amount of quality resources for young people currently available by many of the major Christian publishing companies. One large and helpful line is distributed by the Youth Specialty division of Zondervan. These often have wonderfully creative ideas for engaging youth and children in the reading of the Bible. Or you could create your own curriculum of sorts, such as writing and reading limericks adapted from the Bible! Here are some examples (and resources) to get your young poets started:

God's Care (based on Psalm 23)

The Lord is my shepherd. He leads me.
Beside the still waters He feeds me.
I walk without fear.
Rod and staff show He's near
The feast, at His table, soon will be![2]

Noah's Animals (based on Genesis 7:9)

The bees spent their time making honey.
The squids made some ink black and runny.
The worms made some silk,
The cows made some milk;
The hyenas just thought it all funny.[3]

Sisera's Demise (based on Judges 4:21)

Jael pounded a nail through his head
Until he became rather dead.
She never could sit
To sew or to knit
"But I'm good with a hammer," she said.[4]

INTERGENERATIONAL READING

The typical U.S. church has an average worship attendance of less than a hundred.[5] This means that in many church facilities, most people can easily see each other no matter where in the room they stand.

My coauthor, Warren, belongs to a church with attendance of 150 in a sanctuary that seats 300 maximum. The week we were working on this chapter, the worship service featured a reading from Job 1:1–22. It's the story of Job's world falling apart, and if told well, it conveys a powerful, emotional, and even painful account of loss. It was a great setup for the sermon, which was taken from a different text, but followed that same theme: helping God's people respond to grief and loss.

The reading started like most readings at Warren's church: with a lay reader standing at the podium. A few verses in, when the first actual dialog began, the reader stopped, and voices around the edges of the sanctuary spoke each part of the dialog. There were eight readers involved to cover all of the necessary parts: the narrator, Job, God, Satan, and four different messengers who brought the devastating news to Job. It was evident that the readers had rehearsed their parts, had practiced their reading, and had rehearsed with the tech team before the service. It was equally evident that the congregation was engaged, not just in following a clever approach to reading, but in watching the drama unfold and reflecting on the perspective of all the different players involved.

I describe the reading here because the eight roles were intergenerational. Young people served as the four messengers. This was believable as part of the story, but it also made a statement to everyone present that youth are important at this church and that they're wanted as contributors to the entire church body, not just to their own peer group.

This same intergenerational practice is more natural when families engage the Scriptures together. Warren and I have each seen a Mother's Day reading by a grandmother and her granddaughter. We've experienced Advent readings by family units. A pastor we know asked a different family to read Scripture and lead the congregation in prayer on specific Sunday mornings. This worked really well because children and youth had the support of their families on the platform and in the preparation. "It strengthened the families to serve together," our pastor friend affirmed.

In fact, according to a major research project, families serving together is a significant way of passing along the faith from one generation to another. According to the study, as young adults looked back on their churchgoing childhood, they said the most effective way their parents convinced them of their faith was by acts of service they did, both inside and outside the church.[6] When families read the Word together, it makes a powerful statement to all age groups that the Scriptures are an important and essential part of church life.

CHAPTER ELEVEN

SCRIPTURE READING AT HOME, AT WEDDINGS, AND MORE

AT A RECENT TRAINING CONFERENCE for Scripture readers, one of the speakers described a wedding she had attended where the father of the bride was clearly unhappy with his future son-in-law. Though the prospective groom had tried hard to build a good relationship with his fiancé's father, he had been unsuccessful, even with help from his future wife. On the wedding day, the bride's father was still visibly cold toward his future son-in-law.

Yet, even with the obvious tension between them, the bride's father participated in the wedding ceremony by reading a Scripture passage, honoring a request his daughter had made. The text, often used at weddings, was a reading from 1 Corinthians 13, widely known as the "love chapter."

The father began his reading like many people, reading quickly and obviously self-conscious about the many eyes focused on him. But as he began to read about the characteristics of real love, that love is patient and kind, he began to slow down. When he got to the part in the passage that talks about how love "forgives all things," he paused. And when he read that love "always hopes," he stopped. There was an awkward silence for a few seconds. "I haven't done that," he said, choking back tears and emotion. He then walked over and hugged the young man that was about to become his son-in-law.

The congregation, silent to that point, suddenly broke out in applause as they realized what was happening and saw the genuine reconciliation between the two as they hugged.

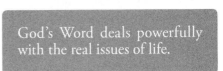

God's Word deals powerfully with the real issues of life.

But it didn't end there. The father went back to the podium where he had been reading. "May I try it again?" he asked his daughter. She nodded with a smile. His voice quivered as he read, "love ... keeps no record of wrongs" (1 Corinthians 13:5), but he made it through the entire narrative.

I imagine that the guests, as they told others about the wedding, all reported the story of how the Bible's message took hold of its reader and transformed a relationship. They had all been reminded that God's Word deals powerfully with the real issues of life.

When we pick up the Word of God, we hold a powerful tool. It is "living and active. Sharper than any double-edged sword, it penetrates even to dividing soul and spirit, joints and marrow; it judges the thoughts and attitudes of the heart" (Hebrews 4:12). Further, God's "word is truth" (John 17:17), it is "flawless"

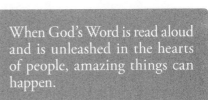

When God's Word is read aloud and is unleashed in the hearts of people, amazing things can happen.

(Psalm 18:30; Proverbs 30:5), and it is a "lamp" and a "light" (Psalm 119:105). It can burn in a believer's heart like a fire (Jeremiah 20:9) or it can cut to the heart of those who don't yet believe (Acts 2:37). It's nothing less than God's voice to us.

When God's Word is read aloud and is unleashed in the hearts of people, amazing things can happen. In one passage of Scripture from the Old Testament, we see that people's hearts were touched by the Word of God and they responded by promising to follow God with all their heart and soul (2 Kings 23:1 – 3). In another situation, the Word made the hearer — a king — so angry that he cut up the scroll with a pocket knife and threw it into a fire! (See Jeremiah 36:21 – 23.) The king was making it clear to all those standing beside him that he wasn't going to respond to God's call to repentance.

Ten Additional Places to Read the Bible Aloud

So far this book has focused mainly on reading Scripture in worship services. However, Scripture reading is not limited to a church's public worship. There are many other places where Scripture can be read aloud and they can be presented with far greater impact. Here are ten of the most common settings.

1. Family Devotions

The Bible is read aloud in millions of homes each day as part of family worship. What if the person doing the reading were to prepare the passage in advance, not as a performance but in a way that would make the reading come more alive for the entire family? Any amount of time that a family spends in the Bible together can be powerful for everyone involved. As

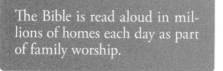

The Bible is read aloud in millions of homes each day as part of family worship.

family members listen to the reading, they have the opportunity to respond, not just as individuals, but in light of their relationships with other family members. A collective response to the Bible can be very convicting for everyone involved.

Chapter 6 ("From Page to Stage") described how to break down your text into thoughts, identify the verbs, let the words speak to you personally, and practice your delivery aloud. The goal is to practice until you feel ready to present the text as if you're having an animated conversation with a good friend. This takes practice and frequent repetition of the passage. I encourage you to read your text aloud at least eight times. Wouldn't it be great if your children or your spouse were to hear the Bible read during your devotion time and feel a deep sense of connection with the text?

Let me offer a few cautions, though, when it comes to doing family devotions. For your devotions, don't merely read good books *about* the Bible. Read the Bible itself. After all, while books about the Bible (including this one) are wonderful aids, they can never replace the Word of God. The Bible itself even encourages us to read it to one another. Ephesians 5:19 commands that we "*speak* to one another with psalms" (emphasis added). Take turns speaking the Word to each other. Try different translations. Experiment with different reading plans until you find one that works best for your family.

Be careful not to place too much emphasis on a specific "mileage" goal, trying to cover so many verses a day. The real goal should be a "content" goal of meeting God afresh in the pages of the Bible and applying those insights to your life. One time-honored approach that I've found helpful goes by the acronym S.O.A.P:

Read the **S**cripture.
Talk about what you **O**bserve.
Apply it to your life.
Pray together.

Our friend Wayne Cordeiro at New Hope Community Church in Honolulu has developed a number of great resources that use the S.O.A.P. approach in daily journaling, individually or as a family. If you are interested in checking those out, visit www.enewhope.org.

2. Reading to Children

Nowadays, it's pretty rare for a child to hear the Bible in school, on television, or through the songs they play on their iPods. Yet we live in a very spiritual time where they are bombarded with a visual and auditory barrage of ideas about God, the supernatural world, and ethical and moral choices. One of the best ways that families can respond to these influences is by beginning or ending each day with some time in God's Word. The frontline of this battle against worldly influence is the family, and the primary way that we fight these influences is through the regular reading of God's Word.

Everyone loves to hear a story, especially children. When you read, show your excitement about the rich characters and the unfolding drama of the Bible, and that passion will soon transfer to your children as you read to them. When God teaches you something through your own Bible reading, share the story of what God did in you with your kids—and then read them the text that God has used to affect your life.

If you read bedtime stories to your children, why not pick some from the Bible as well? If you read them the *Berenstain Bears and the Truth* (Random House, 1983), why not include a compelling story from Scripture about truth, such as the stories found in the *Journey of Jesus*, a book I wrote as a simplified retelling of the New Testament stories.[1] If your children indicate that they and their friends had a discussion about magic, possibly triggered by a Harry Potter or Stephanie Meyer book, try reading them some of the miracles that Jesus did. Your kids may be amazed at how Jesus was able to turn the young boy's few bread loaves and fishes into enough food to feed thousands of hungry people (John 6:1–15)!

Reading the Bible is certainly not limited to your own children. Depending on your situation, there may be opportunities for you to read to your nieces, nephews, or grandchildren. Are there times such as Christmas or Easter when neighborhood children are visiting your home that you could read to them? Are there other children God has brought into your life where it would be appropriate and permissible to read them the Bible? Ask God for opportunities, and don't be surprised when he provides them.

3. Sunday School

George Barna and others have made a strong case that the vast majority of people who make a decision to follow Christ do so before they reach age eighteen. I like the title of his book, *Transforming Children into Spiritual Champions: Why Children Should Be Your Church's #1 Priority.*[2]

Are you a Sunday school director, teacher or helper? As you prepare your lesson, take time to read aloud the Scripture that you will be using, doing so several times to prepare it well.

4. Small Groups

According to a recent survey, 86 percent of churches agreed with the statement that "small groups are central to our strategy for Christian nurture and spiritual formation."[3] Would it be possible to try a more prepared approach to reading the Bible in your small group? Could you model some of the reading methods explained in this book yourself? Could you ask to play one of the segments from the DVD accompanying this book to your small group? You may be able to open the door for some interesting discussions about the ways that people read the Bible and how they are affected by the text.

5. Weddings

The opening story of this chapter was about an unprepared Scripture reader at a wedding. I'm delighted that God worked so wonderfully that time, but sadly, I've been at other weddings where the power of God was hidden by a procedural and lifeless reading of the text.

If you've been asked to do a reading for a wedding, or if you're involved in planning a wedding, put the principles of this book to work in the preparation. See the Quick-Start Guide (chapter 8) as a good place for some tips on how to prepare. Do you have a wedding planner at your church who helps plan weddings? Why not show that person this book and DVD as a way of beginning the conversation?

6. Funerals

The same idea applies to funerals, where family members or church leaders often read a passage of Scripture. Your tone and passion level need to match the mood of the occasion, but even at funerals,

> None of us ever reaches the point where we no longer need to encounter God through his Word.

where we think about eternal life, no one wants to hear a life*less* reading of God's Word!

7. Hospital Visitation

In 2005, during the final moments of Pope John Paul II's life, tens of thousands crowded St. Peter's Square while those closest to the pope gathered around his bedside, bidding farewell to their mentor and leader of the church. Among the pope's last words was a simple request: "Read me the Bible." One of the priests serving him gladly obliged, reading him nine chapters from the gospel according to St. John.

In 2008, at Billy Graham's ninetieth birthday, what did he want to hear? His grandchildren reading him the Bible.

None of us, no matter how old or how involved in spiritual work, ever reaches the point where we no longer need to encounter God through his Word.

My wife, Sharon, and I have visited many people in the hospital over the years, and from time to time have read them a Scripture passage. Warren and his wife, Michelle, have done the same. In most cases, when given permission to read, people appreciate it greatly, and the hearing often elicits tears. Often, people in hospitals are more open and spiritually vulnerable, and they want to hear from God. Hospital visits are a great opportunity to read from God's Word.

If you are planning on picking out a passage in advance of your visit, why not practice it as well? Read it aloud eight times, at first slowly, looking for the thought blocks, verbs, and personal applications to your own life, just as if you are preparing to read at church. See if you can tell any difference in how it's received if you prepare it well. Here are some

passages you might consider for reading in a hospital setting, adapted
from Zondervan's Bible Reference software:

- *If you feel despair*—Psalm 119:116; Isaiah 57:15; Jeremiah 32:17;
  Hebrews 10:35
- *If you are depressed*—Deuteronomy 31:8; Psalm 34:18; Isaiah
  49:13–15; Romans 5:5
- *If you are anxious*—Psalm 55:22; Isaiah 41:13; Matthew 6:25;
  Matthew 11:28–29; Philippians 4:6–7; 1 Peter 5:7
- *If you are filled with longing*—Psalm 37:4; Psalm 84:11; Psalm
  103:5; Luke 12:29–31
- *If you are sick*—Psalm 23:4; Psalm 73:26; Isaiah 57:18; Mat-
  thew 8:16–17; John 16:33; Romans 8:37–39; James 5:14–15
- *If you are afraid*—Psalm 4:8; Psalm 23:4; Isaiah 35:4; Romans
  8:37–39; 2 Corinthians 1:10; 2 Timothy 1:7; Hebrews 13:6
- *If you are in need*—Isaiah 58:11; John 6:35; 2 Corinthians
  9:10–11; Ephesians 3:20–21; Philippians 4:19
- *If you grieve*—Psalm 119:50, 76–77; Jeremiah 31:13; Matthew
  5:4; John 16:20–22; 1 Thessalonians 4:13–14; Revelation 21:3–4
- *If you suffer*—Psalm 34:19; Nahum 1:7; John 16:33; Romans
  8:16–17; 1 Peter 2:20–21; 1 Peter 4:12–13
- *If the future seems hopeless*—Isaiah 54:1–7; Lamentations
  3:19–24; 1 Corinthians 15:20–28; 1 Peter 1:1–9; 1 Peter
  5:10–11; Revelation 11:15–19
- *If you are seeking God's direction*—1 Kings 3:1–14; Proverbs 2:1–6; Romans 12:1–3; Ephesians 5:15–17; Colossians
  1:9–14; James 1:5–8
- *If you need comfort*—Isaiah 12; Isaiah 40:1–11; Jeremiah
  31:10–13; 2 Corinthians 1:3–7; 2 Corinthians 7:6- 13
- *If your faith needs strengthening*—Genesis 15:1–6; Proverbs 3:5-
  9; Romans 5:1–11; 1 Corinthians 9:24–27; Hebrews 10:19–25,
  35–39; Hebrews 11:1–12:13
- *If you are challenged by dark forces*—Joshua 1:6–9; Psalm
  56:1–4; Romans 8:38–39; 2 Corinthians 4:7–18; Ephesians
  6:10–18; 2 Timothy 4:6–7
- *If you struggle with addiction*—Psalm 18:28–36; Proverbs
  23:29–35; Romans 6:1–23; Romans 12:1–2; 1 Corinthians
  6:12–20; Philippians 3:17–4:1
- *If you desire to learn how to pray*—2 Chronicles 6:13–42;
  2 Chronicles 20:5–12; Matthew 6:5–15; Mark 11:22–25; Luke
  18:9–14; Philippians 4:4–7

8. Retreats

Many churches sponsor spiritual retreats for everyone from youth to adults. Often there are meetings that include the public reading of Scripture. What would happen if a team of people took responsibility for the main Bible reading, practicing it and planning some way to present it not only passionately, but creatively as well?

9. Oral Interpretation Classes

For centuries, the Bible served as a school textbook for teaching people the basics of reading and writing. People would learn to read by hearing the Bible read aloud, and then would use the Bible to practice reading for themselves. In fact, America's first Bible was printed for that purpose — John Eliot's *Algonquin Indian Bible* of 1663 — designed both for evangelizing and for teaching Algonquins to read.

In 1782 the United States Congress authorized printing of the first English Bible printed in America, known as the *Aitken Bible*, which schools used widely as a reading primer. Today, for many missionaries working with people groups who do not have a written language, the Bible is the first book printed in written form. By translating the Bible, these missionaries are both preserving their culture (by helping them put their language in written form) and also presenting the Word of God to the people.[4]

Many high schools, colleges, and universities have courses like "The Bible as Literature." There are frequently opportunities to practice reading the Bible aloud in a classroom setting. Other courses, such as "Oral Interpretation," often use sections from the Bible to practice various readings and to receive expert coaching at it. After all, the Bible is the world's bestselling and most-owned book year after year. And Christians would say it's more than a bestselling book; it's the world's best book period!

10. Reading Marathons

Your local newspaper probably runs at least one article a year on some group, locally or nationally, that reads the Bible aloud cover to cover in a public event. Maybe it's a youth group adventure. Or perhaps it's a way of dedicating a new worship facility, commemorating National Bible week (www.nationalbible.org), or affirming the role the Bible has played in the founding and development of this nation. Did you know, for example, that each year at the U.S. Capitol building there is a Bible Reading Marathon (www.dcbiblemarathon.org), sponsored by the International Bible Reading Association? It's done as a lead-up to the annual National Day of Prayer.

It takes, by the way, between sixty and seventy-five hours to cover the entire Bible aloud, but massive events like the one above usually allot ninety hours.

There's an excellent, detailed guide on how to conduct a Bible reading marathon on the website of The International Bible Reading Association (www.internationalbiblereadingassociation.org). If you are considering hosting a Bible reading event of this type, here are a few items to consider, adopted from their materials:

- *Platform or stand for readers*—Provide an extra stool or platform for small readers, especially if you have children involved. A platform is a good place to display your banner and any other type of decorations you may want.
- *Podium*—If possible, set up two lecterns, one for the current reader; the other for the next reader, to avoid delays. Each lectern should have a good microphone attached to it.
- *Bible*—Have large or giant print Bibles available for easier reading, but encourage readers to bring their own personal Bibles. Some marathons have had readers read their own Bibles in different languages, which can be an encouragement to illustrate that the Word of God is being proclaimed and is applicable and relevant in every language. If your marathon is being conducted in a multinational area, you may wish to provide Bibles in various languages.
- *Sound system*—Your sound system should have sufficient volume and quality if you are having your marathon outside. The entire public address system, including the microphones, must be carefully tested and finely tuned ahead of time. If any of your microphones require batteries, have replacements on hand.
- *Lighting system*—This should be adequate for night reading. Having good lighting is also a safety measure. Include spare light bulbs.
- *Electrical outlets*—Make sure there are enough outlets for amplifiers, lighting, and the like. Also check that your location has ample wattage available to plug in all necessary equipment. Be sure all outlets are protected from the elements.
- *Banner or identifying sign*—A waterproof banner is best. Think hard about the wording you want on the banner, as many people will see it.

- *Seating*—You will want chairs for those who are participating and for groups waiting to read, as well as sufficient chairs for spectators.
- *Umbrellas, water jugs, cups, etc.*—Have these items all located in one spot, off to the side and out of the way. Oversize umbrellas are a great help in rainy conditions!
- *Refreshments*—Providing refreshments for readers is a nice touch of hospitality and a good place to strike up informal conversations. A caterer or restaurant might be willing to contribute this free of charge.
- *Large plastic bags*—Have several on hand that are large enough to cover sound equipment if it should rain. You will also need a few trash bags during and after the Marathon. We represent Christ and need to leave the reading area cleaner than when we began.
- *Small emergency kit*—Keep a first aid kit handy, just in case of minor accidents.
- *Camera, video, etc.*—You may need to obtain a special permit if you plan to use photographers or video cameras. Check this out well in advance.
- *Telephone*—It is wise to have cell phone(s) available for security purposes, with various emergency numbers handy, as well as for coordinators and media people.
- *Thank-you list.* Be sure to publicly acknowledge those businesses and/or organizations that have helped supply equipment, refreshments, and other items for the Marathon.

WHEREVER YOU READ, LOOK FOR GOD TO CHANGE YOU AS WELL

The goal of any reading of Scripture is the transformation of both reader and listener. Consider the story of Philip and the Ethiopian in Acts 8:26–39. Notice how God was able to work as the Ethiopian was reading the Bible out loud. Not only was the Ethiopian official changed by the experience of reading God's Word, but Philip also had a powerful encounter with God's Spirit.

> Now an angel of the Lord said to Philip, "Go south to the road—the desert road—that goes down from Jerusalem to Gaza." So he started

out, and on his way he met an Ethiopian eunuch, an important official in charge of all the treasury of Candace, queen of the Ethiopians. This man had gone to Jerusalem to worship, and on his way home was sitting in his chariot reading the book of Isaiah the prophet. The Spirit told Philip, "Go to that chariot and stay near it."

Then Philip ran up to the chariot and heard the man reading Isaiah the prophet. "Do you understand what you are reading?" Philip asked.

"How can I," he said, "unless someone explains it to me?" So he invited Philip to come up and sit with him.

The eunuch was reading this passage of Scripture:

"He was led like a sheep to the slaughter,
   and as a lamb before the shearer is silent,
   so he did not open his mouth.
In his humiliation he was deprived of justice.
   Who can speak of his descendants?
   For his life was taken from the earth."

The eunuch asked Philip, "Tell me, please, who is the prophet talking about, himself or someone else?" Then Philip began with that very passage of Scripture and told him the good news about Jesus.

As they traveled along the road, they came to some water and the eunuch said, "Look, here is water. Why shouldn't I be baptized?" And he gave orders to stop the chariot. Then both Philip and the eunuch went down into the water and Philip baptized him. When they came up out of the water, the Spirit of the Lord suddenly took Philip away, and the eunuch did not see him again, but went on his way rejoicing.

Scripture Is Essential to Build a Community of Faith

During Bible times, the oral reading of Scripture was vital to building up the community of faith. This can be seen throughout the New Testament (Luke 4:16–22; Colossians 4:16–17; 1 Thessalonians 5:27; 1 Timothy 4:13; etc.). The practice stems from Jewish history such as this ancient instruction given to Israel:

These commandments that I give you today are to be upon your *hearts*. Impress them on your *children*. Talk about them when you *sit at home and when you walk along the road, when you lie down and when you get up.* Tie them as symbols on your hands and bind them on your foreheads. *Write them on the doorframes of your houses* and on your gates. (Deuteronomy 6:6–9, emphasis added)

This oft-quoted passage affirms that our Bible reading is not to be limited to the privacy of our "prayer closet" equivalents. We are to take it with us wherever we go.

Paul wrote, "All Scripture is God-breathed and is useful for teaching, rebuking, correcting and training in righteousness, *so that the man of God may be thoroughly equipped for every good work*" (2 Timothy 3:16–17, emphasis added).

> During Bible times, the oral reading of Scripture was vital to building up the community of faith.

Paul also instructed Timothy, a young preacher he was apprenticing, to "devote" himself to "the public reading of Scripture" (1 Timothy 4:13). We need to find appropriate ways to go public with God's powerful Word.

May God's people be better equipped every time you read, whatever the context!

PART FOUR

NEXT STEPS

Chapter Twelve

What to Do Next

Unleashing the Word is about awakening the passion contained in any text of the Bible as it is read aloud, whether you read at church, at home, in a small group, or for a special occasion. It encourages you to let the text speak to you so that it will speak *through* you to others. It invites you to use the tools of oral interpretation in a way that's natural and organic in whatever setting you do the reading.

Scripture reading is often not done well, and poor readings convey to listeners that the text is not important. In the context of a worship service, the reading is seen as a prelude to the real deal — the sermon.

The fruits of these poor readings are many. The passage doesn't penetrate the heart, mind, or soul of those listening. It invites people to tune out the Word of God. It discourages personal reading of the Bible because the text seems boring and inaccessible. In a church context, it does little to help prepare people spiritually to receive the message of the sermon or to experience the Lord's table.

For many people, the public reading of Scripture in church is the primary way they experience the Bible being read out loud. As a result, even though the Bible is available in a variety of formats, many people today don't realize the powerful promise God makes about his Word when it is unleashed:

> As the rain and the snow
>   come down from heaven,
> and do not return to it
>   without watering the earth

and making it bud and flourish,
>> so that it yields seed for the sower and bread for the eater,
> so is my word that goes out from my mouth:
>> It will not return to me empty,
> but will accomplish what I desire
>> and achieve the purpose for which I sent it.
> You will go out in joy
>> and be led forth in peace;
> the mountains and hills
>> will burst into song before you,
> and all the trees of the field
>> will clap their hands. (Isaiah 55:10 – 12)

People in our churches need to hear the life-changing message of the Bible read in a way that communicates the truth with power.

When the Bible is read well, it conveys a penetrating power as the Holy Spirit brings the text to life in the hearts of those listening. There is energy as the Word is spoken out loud. Good reading evokes in us a deeper desire to know God. It awakens spiritual passion, creates curiosity, and develops our faith. As Scripture affirms, "faith comes from hearing ... the word" (Romans 10:17).

Good reading evokes in us a deeper desire to know God. It awakens spiritual passion, creates curiosity, and develops our faith.

THREE STEPS

Recently I heard Andy Crouch, an insightful writer on culture, speak to a group at my church. Stimulated by what he said, I read his book called *Culture Making*.[1] It's an excellent manifesto that calls Christians not to condemn culture, critique it, copy it, or consume it so much as to use their influence and creativity to *shape* culture by creating *new* culture.

Andy's focus is largely on the world outside the church as Christians impact the greater society. I wanted Andy's take on changing the culture (the way things are done) inside a church, such as the attitudes, practices, and general atmosphere about how Scripture is read.

"Suppose," I asked him, "the regular practice at a church is for the Bible to be read poorly—in a procedural, rather expressionless, detached way. What would a pastor or reading team need to keep in mind as they transition the culture to one of a more prepared, heartfelt, and engaged style of reading?"

He said the basic process of changing the way things are done in a church's worship is the same as introducing change into wider society. Andy's advice boils down to three helpful steps.

1. Create Something New

You need to model the better way, which then gives people imagination about alternatives to what they've experienced in the past. Culture changes only if you introduce a new cultural good—what sociologists call artifacts. As Andy says in his book:

> The only way to change culture is to create more of it.... If culture is to change, it will be because something ... begins to reshape their world.... Cultural change will only happen when something new displaces, to some extent, existing culture in a very tangible way.... No matter how much we may protest ... unless we offer an alternative, the show will go on [in the same way as before]."[2]

2. Don't Do It Too Fast

Cultures resist rapid, dramatic change, so it's always right to ask, what are the incremental changes we could make that would lead the culture in the way we want to go?

You might start with something as simple as the people who are already reading Scripture. Ask them to read this book and then get together to talk about it. You might introduce a new reader to your lineup, someone with both a heart for God and also an ear and knack for storytelling. That person may help elicit a higher quality of reading.

3. Interpret the Change for People As It Happens

Put it in a broader framework, showing why it matters. Perhaps underscore some of the points made in this book, using some of the scriptural illustrations we use. Maybe you can also draw from church history and your congregation's specific history. Affirm that you're not changing the "what" (the public reading of God's Word), just the "how"—and elevating how the "what" comes across.

Whatever you do, it's essential to link the change with kingdom values. Repeatedly affirm how a different approach to Bible reading will foster more biblical values.

Culture Shifting

My coauthor, Warren Bird, contributed to a book with a title similar to the book by Andy Crouch, but one that approaches the idea of changing the culture from a slightly different angle. *Culture Shift,* by Robert Lewis, Wayne Cordeiro, and Warren Bird, tells the story of two different churches, showing how their pastors (Lewis and Cordeiro) identified the internal culture of the congregation, determined what shifts were necessary, and then led their congregations through appropriate transitions to get there.

Their insights on being change agents in a divine partnership are applicable to anyone who wants to help improve the way Scripture reading is done in their church or group. The entire book is excellent, but these two insights seem especially relevant:

- "A chorus is always better than a solo in setting culture."[3]
- "You release culture through people. Spiritually energized people *are* the convincing point in a culturally healthy congregation."[4]

In short, when God is behind a change in how his Word is read, you can look around and expect to find allies. The most important allies you can have at church are your pastor and worship leadership. Partner with them to influence others, go slowly and gradually, and repeatedly demonstrate the kingdom values that are resulting.

I started the Scripture reading group at my church in 2002. I've seen and felt the intensity and quality of listening to the public reading of the Scripture grow by leaps and bounds. There is an expectation that God will speak through his Word, and the connection between the sermon and the Scripture is more evident. I can sense the satisfaction in an artistic sense that comes from the joy expressed from those who receive the Scripture and from those who deliver it. It is a public manifestation that "God is really among [us]" (1 Corinthian 14:25).

May God likewise lead you to discover the penetrating power of his Word, and then to make compelling presentations that will evoke a deeper desire to know God, both for yourself and for all who experience your readings.

CHAPTER THIRTEEN

Q&A WITH MAX MCLEAN

HERE ARE THE QUESTIONS I receive most frequently when I dialog with Scripture readers or prospective Scripture readers.

1. How can I learn the right way to pronounce the names of people or places in the passage I'm planning to read?

I'm not sure there is always a single "right" pronunciation. For example, how do you pronounce *Peniel*, the place where Jacob wrestled with the angel of the Lord (see Genesis 32)? Do you want to say it the way the ancient Hebrews pronounced it? Or should you pronounce it the way an Israeli would say it in modern Hebrew? There's no consensus on how to americanize the word. I've heard *PEN-nee-el, Pen-NILE,* and *Pen-YEL.*

Go online to www.biblegateway.com and listen online to how others pronounce it (Catholics might go to www.usccb.org/nab). Or use a Bible translation that has pronunciation marks. Some regular readers might purchase a pronunciation guide or Bible dictionary (see chapter 9 for more specific help with pronunciation guides). Sometimes it's appropriate to ask your pastor if you think the hard-to-pronounce term will show up in what is said in the teaching.

Whatever pronunciation you select, read it with confidence. Otherwise your hesitation will draw attention to the word in question and become distracting.

2. *What if I make a mistake, such as skipping or stumbling over a word?*

It's usually best to correct yourself and move on. Briefly pause, and then say the word or phrase again. For example, "At the beginning, God created." *Pause, collect yourself, and begin again.* "In the beginning God created the heavens and the earth" (Genesis 1:1).

Do as little as possible to draw attention to yourself or the error. I would avoid being wordy, jokey, or self-focused, like, "Oops, looks like I goofed. Ha Ha."

3. *What Bible translation should I use?*

If there's a "standard" translation in your church or group, use it — or ask permission before shifting to another translation. You want your reading to fit into the existing culture, so that people's attention goes to the Word, not to you and not to a distracting thought, such as, "What translation is *that*?" If it's appropriate to select from a variety of translations, then choose one that your church's leadership feels comfortable with or, better, the actual version that your pastor is preaching from, and reference it as you begin. "I'm reading Psalm 100 from the New American Standard Bible."

4. *How much transition time should I allow before I start my reading?*

Try to minimize the "wait time" whenever appropriate. Too often the transition time runs so long that people lose attention. This usually happens by accident. Suppose the Scripture reading occurs after a song. A reader may wait until the vocalists completely exit or sit down, and then at that point will stand up, walk up to the platform, adjust the microphone and reading materials, focus, and then start. This set of activities might keep the reader fully occupied, but for everyone else it's usually not worship — it's dead time.

5. *Do most people read too fast or too slow?*

Too fast. Nervousness causes most people to speed up. The harm in reading too fast is that you slide over too many important words or concepts, and your hearers receive only a tiny portion of the impact God's Word can have.

Likewise, sometimes readers are self-conscious about their reading speed and they try to follow the example of a fast-talking radio announcer in order to prevent hearers' minds from wandering. That's usually not a good model to follow. Rather imagine a setting where you have something important to say—a carefully thought-out message to your boss or perhaps even a marriage proposal. In those cases you want to speak in such a way that every word you say matters!

6. *Many times two people, such as a husband and wife, will be asked to read Scripture at church. What creative touches can be done, other than for one person to read the first half and the second person to read the rest?*

While creativity is often helpful, take care to avoid being gimmicky or cutesy. Each person should be responsible to give the best reading of their part of the Scripture. Start your preparation by breaking the assigned text into specific thought groups, and then try to experience the text personally: what is it really saying, and how does that impact you? At that point, you can discuss whether there are groupings or emphases that lend themselves to a back-and-forth reading style between two people. The primary objective is not to be creative. It is on how best to communicate the meaning of the Scripture.

7. *When someone reads, there are several ways we can follow—reading along out loud, following silently in our own Bibles or worship guide, following the words projected on screens behind the reader, or simply listening without seeing the words anywhere. Which is best?*

It depends on the culture of your church. The question to ask is: What will lead to the greatest personal understanding of the text by the congregation? It is true that most people comprehend best by combining multiple senses, such as both hearing and seeing. But sometimes the effort to follow along or read in unison is more distracting than the benefit that comes from doing so.

8. *In some churches, the entire congregation reads a passage together, such as using a pew Bible or following a PowerPoint projection. What tips could you give a layperson who guides the congregation in that kind of group reading?*

Prepare carefully, just as if you'll be reading it solo. Set the pace for the congregation by reading slowly and expressively. You probably won't be able to have the same full range of rate and volume changes as you could if reading alone, but you can still bring out the emphases that impressed you as you studied and practiced the text.

Remember too that not everyone reads aloud, even when invited to do so. Many will listen, both to the person next to them and to your voice as amplified by the sound system.

9. *It seems that more and more laypeople are serving as the Scripture readers at church. Why can they do as good a job, or sometimes better, than a seminary-trained, ordained minister?*

The important thing is that the reading is done well. The public reading of Scripture should be treated with the same importance as the selection of a singer in worship: find people with the right heart and the ability to articulate well. Some pastors are naturally gifted in reading aloud, though only a few have received special training in how to read Scripture aloud, as seminaries focus almost exclusively on sermon preparation and preaching rather than on reading aloud.

10. *What could the Scripture reader or readers' group say when they're done? It seems too routine or mechanical always to conclude a reading with the same expression, such as, "This is the Word of the Lord."*

In general, say as little as possible. See Appendix A for ideas of some short concluding phrases.

11. *Should I state the verse numbers as I read?*

It's usually helpful to introduce the source of your reading as you begin, "Today's Scripture comes from 1 Peter 2:1 – 12," but don't itemize each verse during the actual reading. Chapter and verse dividers were not part of the original Bible; they were added centuries later. More important, it distracts from the content when you insert the words "verse 9," then "verse 10," then "verse 11" and so forth.

12. *I don't want to come across as if I am selling something. How do I read with feeling, but not so much emotion that I sound over the top?*

It's normal to guard against a sense of overselling a text. Don't back off so much that you do the opposite, however. Usually the bigger problem is underselling because readers are afraid to commit, and the words stay flat on the page. Err on the side of showing too much energy; chances are, this will lead you to express just the right amount of energy.

13. *Should I mark the text I'm to read with printed cues to remind me when to pause, gesture, look up, breath, or emphasize a certain word? If yes, what's a good way to do so?*

Most readers do print out their text and mark different emphases on it. Commonly used tools are underlines or circles around words or phrases, small check marks for breathing (as singers often employ), exclamation marks (!), or vertical bars ||| for short pauses — the more bars, the longer the pause.

I did not emphasize these techniques in this book because my passion has been to cultivate authentic reading that avoids the ring of anything hollow or rote. Written cues certainly don't cause hollow readings, but they may tempt people to take shortcuts that avoid genuinely encountering the passage.

14. *What does it look like when I'm combining together all the training and advice in this book?*

You'll have a sense of expressing your inmost being, and you'll know that you are able to convey that blessing to others. You'll read the way you talk, as if it's an animated conversation (though with virtually no hand gestures) with a good friend. God's Word will dwell richly in you (Colossians 3:16) and as you read it, it will not "return ... empty" (Isaiah 55:10–11).

THINGS YOU MIGHT SAY BEFORE OR AFTER READING

OFTEN, READERS WONDER WHAT THEY SHOULD SAY before and after the actual reading of a Scripture passage. In general, it is always best to err by saying too little rather than too much. If you are directed by the liturgy or your pastor to say something, please follow the guidance that they give you. If you are not given a pattern or if there isn't a set model of how other readers at your church introduce their readings, you can try adapting one of the following lines:

"Our reading is from [TEXT], which is page [NUMBER] in your pew Bibles."

"Today's reading comes from [TEXT], which is printed in your worship guide (or on the screen above me)."

"Today's reading comes from [TEXT], using the New International Version."

"I'll be reading [TEXT], and I invite you to follow along in your own Bibles. Please stand for the reading of God's Word."

After you finish reading the assigned text, should you add a concluding or transitional statement? It is usually best to ask your pastor or worship leader for guidance on what is most appropriate for your church's worship setting. If they feel it is appropriate and give permission, here are some things you might say as a way of concluding the reading:

"This is the reading of God's Word."

"This is the Word of the Lord."

"May God's Word fill your life and light your world."

"May we now 'walk before God in the light of life'" [from Psalm 56:13, NIV].

"May God bless *you* as you reflect on His Word."

"May God add a blessing to the reading of His Word."

If there are no guidelines, again, remember that less is more — even if your church is highly relational and informal in its style. If you choose to personalize your reading by stating your name or saying "Good morning," remember to keep the spotlight on God's Word — not on the personality of God's messenger!

How I Prepare a Scripture Reading

MY MOST RECENT READING ASSIGNMENT at church was Romans 3:21–31.

I start with prayer. I ask God to speak his Word through me. I ask God to work through me as his "ambassador" (see 2 Corinthians 5:20) for his glory, for my edification, and for the benefit of my listeners.

After prayer, I normally begin my preparation by printing out the passage, double-spaced, grabbing a pencil, and finding a cozy chair to sit in. For my first reading, I go through the entire assigned passage—all 230 or so words in the New International Version. It is simply an oral recitation of the text; I just need to get the words out of my mouth so I can hear them and get a sense of what I'm dealing with. At this point I don't invest a lot of emotional energy in the reading. To be honest, I wouldn't have even known where to put my energy or what to do with it. Besides, too much emotion without really knowing the text just comes across as false and hammy. Still, this initial reading is quite flat and boring. Unfortunately, this is where most people not only begin, but also end with the text.

The initial reading seeks to get the lay of the land. My first impression is that this will be a tough assignment. I think to myself: *I'm really going to have to work hard to draw out the argument that Paul is making so that it is clear and understandable while also conveying the urgency and passion that Paul is feeling as he writes.*

I begin my second reading more carefully, slowly, and intently. The first thing I do is break the opening verse into thought groups. Since people receive information one thought at a time, when I break sentences up into thoughts, I am beginning to think about how people receive the words and thoughts that I am voicing.

I use slash marks to show how I break up the first verse into distinct thought units: "But now / a righteousness from God, / apart from law, / has been made known, / to which the Law and the Prophets testify" (Romans 3:21).

At the same time, I also begin to think about meaning and flow. Those two opening words, "but now," suggest that something new is emerging. What is Paul saying here? What is this new idea?

My next read of the verse focuses on finding the verbs. Verbs move the action forward. So this time I emphasize and ponder the words in boldface: "But now / a righteousness from God, / apart from law, / **has been made known**, / to which the Law and the Prophets testify."

In this case the verb is a phrase: "has been made known." The subject is righteousness. The stripped-down core idea is that a righteousness, different than the righteousness that we understand, has been made known. In other words, a righteousness that has always existed is now being declared. When I speak the verb "has been made known," I must get this idea of a fresh or new declaration across to my listeners.

Righteousness is the subject. That's what Paul is teaching about. So the phrase "righteousness" has to be communicated with an inflection or energy that triggers this idea in the hearers and reminds them that this is the controlling idea or concept. The "righteousness" that Paul is explaining is qualified as being "apart from law." In other words, law is the *former* righteousness. The new righteousness that Paul is talking about — the "but now" righteousness of the passage — was *testified to* "by the Law and the Prophets." Why is *that* important? I suspect that in Paul's time, every one of his listeners was looking to the Law and Prophets as the authoritative standard of God's goodness and justice. And it's true! The Law and the Prophets do, indeed, point to the righteousness that Paul is describing. In other words, Paul is not making up a *new* religion. He is revealing a true righteousness that the "Law and the Prophets" long ago talked about or pointed to — a righteousness that they testified to, but *one that is only now being revealed*.

Now that I grasp the meaning of this verse, I am ready to go to the next verse. Here we find even more information to process and build upon. I break the next verse into four bite-size thought groups: "This righteousness from God / comes through faith / in Jesus Christ / to all who believe" (Romans 3:22).

As I did with the first verse, I isolate the subject "righteousness" and the verb "comes." The verb "comes" gives the verse its power. It moves the listener to the source of this newly revealed righteousness — "faith." But this is not just any old faith. It is a very specific type of faith. It is faith in Jesus Christ. But that's not the only qualifier! This faith is also associated with an action: *to all who believe*. I want my listeners to hear and appreciate how important believing is to the process of attaining righteousness.

Moving forward, I look at the next sentence, which spans three verses. "There is no difference, / for all have sinned / and fall short of the glory of God, / and are justified freely / by his grace / through the redemption / that came by Christ Jesus" (Romans 3:22–24).

The first thought contains the word "no." I often find the word "no" (or "yes," for that matter) to be an important word to emphasize. I take note of that in my reading notes for the phrase "there is no difference." Again, where is the verb in this verse? "Sinned" is the verb. Who or what is the subject? "All" of us are the subject; we "all" have sinned. "All" is such a comprehensive word that it can't be minimized in this context. It, too, will require emphasis. The next verb, "fall," is modified by the word "short." All "fall short." Of what? "The glory of God."

I move to the second half of this sentence, which begins in verse 24, using the word "and." I am typically wary about overemphasizing the word *and*, but in this case it is certainly deserved. The previous sentence leaves us falling short. "And" tells us that the story isn't over! What follows is vitally important. "And" we are *justified freely*. Justified is the action. Freely modifies the justification in a wonderful way. We are justified *freely*. We are not justified begrudgingly. Rather, it is a prodigious outpouring of justification that we have received by two things: "by his grace" and "through the redemption" that "came" from—Christ Jesus.

Whew! There it is. I am getting somewhere now. This takes work!

As you can see, it takes some careful spade work to really dig into the Scripture. This is the digging I do in preparation for reading that allows me to have a conversation with Scripture. I talk to the Scriptures and the Scriptures talk to me. This is active, fruitful meditation that warms my heart and builds my confidence that what I will say for God will make a difference. As a reader for others, I am an ambassador, representing God and his message to the people listening. I keep this in mind as I study how to deliver this verse with the right phrasing and the appropriate energy.

So far, I've broken down all the sentences into distinct thoughts. I've used a pencil to make a / or | mark between each thought group. I know what the subject is, "righteousness." I've circled some of the verbs. I've reflected on adverbs like "justified *freely*" that add color and texture to my delivery. I've felt myself well up with passion for what I am saying. I'm beginning to see the emotional journey of this text, all the while interacting personally with it and letting it interact with me.

> I'm beginning to see the emotional journey of this text, all the while interacting personally with it and letting it interact with me.

My spadework isn't quite as linear as I'm making it sound, but it does follow a general progression: I read the text to get the big picture, I break it up into thoughts, and I look at each word, especially the verbs.

At the same time, I want the text to speak to me. That's the primary goal. I try to apply the Word to myself, personally engaging with it each time I read—even if it's just a verse or two. Only then can I begin to think about flow—how to make the peaks, valleys, nooks, and crannies all fit together into a seamless whole that weaves the thoughts together.

As I've been preparing this passage, some of my readings have been silent interactions with specific moments of the text. But most of the time, I've read out loud, even transitioning from a rote reading into a full articulation of the passage as I experiment vocally with some different ways of conveying the nuances of meaning. Always remember that as the reader, simply understanding the text is not enough. Good preparation requires that you get the words out of your mouth and into the ears of those listening. To help me in the actual delivery of the passage, I usually make various marks on my printout, placing a check mark at a location in the passage where I might need to draw a breath. (This accumulation of cues is why most people print out the verses.)

After I've repeatedly gone through the entire passage, I am now ready to put it together into an animated conversation. Some people find a mirror helpful at this point, but I don't personally use one. When I say "animated," I'm not interested in physical hand gestures. I'm talking about being *vocally* animated. I'll practice speaking the passage until my technique is so embedded in my read that neither I nor my listeners will be hearing my technique; they'll be listening to what I'm saying. Or better, they will sense that I am having an energetic conversation *with* them.

As I've followed this process with different Scripture readings over the years, it has become more and more intuitive. Every time I practice, the Word of God connects with my soul in a fresh way. I'm learning to speak the Scriptures in ways that connect to other people and touch their soul. With each reading, I grow in confidence that my meditation in the Word will cause other people to experience God himself—his transcendence—as they hear it spoken aloud. Elevating God's Word is a most fulfilling and joyful task.

Suggested Texts for Practice

HERE ARE A FEW GOOD PASSAGES TO PRACTICE WITH. They are read often and illustrate different reading styles. However, the approach in our Quick-Start Guide (chapter 8) will work well for any of these styles.

Genesis 1:26–2:3
Often read at weddings; a good combination of narrative and poetry.

Psalm 23:1–6
Often read at funerals. It's important to work through it so that the read is "yours." Many times you will hear a reading of it in your mind and automatically try to emulate that. Make sure to go through the steps and make it your own. It will then have more impact on those who hear it.

John 1:1–18
A difficult read but one that rewards the work that you put into it. It is simply magnificent when done well. If Jesus has become overly familiar to you or your hearers, this text will bring out the majesty and awe of Jesus. The text will make you work through Jesus' eternal glory and his amazing humility.

Luke 2:8–20
A great read for Christmas. It is an exciting narrative with many emotional transitions within the arc of this familiar story. Take the time to work through this so you feel it. Then let loose.

1 Corinthians 13:1–13
One of my favorite passages to read. It never fails to convict and overwhelm me. It is often read at weddings. The way love is described will not fail to melt the heart because the more you slow down and take the time to engage each description of love (make each one a thought group), the more compelling and emotional this passage will become.

Revelation 21:1–7
Often read at funerals. This has a similar impact to 1 Corinthians 13 at weddings—very moving and hope filled. Be sure to take time to feel it and engage.

RESOURCES AVAILABLE FROM MAX MCLEAN

May be ordered online at www.listenersbible.com or by phone at 888.876.5661.

BIBLES

- *The Listener's NIV Bible on CD: New International Version*; 66-CD set, 77 hours; zippered leatherette case and track booklet.
- *The Listener's ESV Bible on CD: English Standard Version*; 62-CD set, 75 hours; zippered leatherette case and track booklet.
- *The Listener's KJV Bible on CD: King James Version*; 65-CD set, 80 hours; zippered leatherette case and track booklet.
- *The Listener's NIV MP3 Bible*: 4-CD set, 77 hours; complete Bible.
- *The Listener's ESV MP3 Bible*: 4-CD set, 75 hours; complete Bible.
- *The Listener's KJV MP3 Bible*: 4-CD set, 80 hours; complete Bible.
- *The Listener's NIV New Testament with Psalms & Proverbs*: 22-CD set, 25 hours; two favorite Old Testament books accompany the New Testament in this product.
- *The Listener's ESV New Testament*: 15-CD set, 18 hours; New Testament books only.
- *The Listener's KJV New Testament*: 15-CD set, 19 hours; New Testament books only.
- *The Listener's NIV Go Bible*: this pocket–sized digital player is preloaded with the NIV translation and is searchable down to the verse.
- *The Listener's NIV Bible on DVD*: text and video are synched for the ease of reading along as Max McLean narrates the NIV Bible. Perfect for PC or large screen TV viewing.
- *Genesis DVD and Mark's Gospel DVD*: Bible stories are brought to life as you watch the DVDs of Max McLean's live stage performances of Genesis and Mark's Gospel.

- *John's Gospel*: 2-CD set of the Book of John (NIV)
- *Mark's Gospel*: 2-CD set of the Book of Mark (NIV)
- *Revelation*: 1 CD (Holman Christian Standard Bible translation)
- *Romans*: 1 CD (ESV)
- *The Promise of Christmas*: 1 CD; this magnificent CD unites Scripture in the KJV and inspiring music featuring orchestra, brass ensemble, harp, classical guitar and soloist, and choir, all telling the story of God's gift to humankind.
- *His Christmas Story*: 1 CD; feel the weight of this extraordinary event in this 25-minute Scripture CD that explores the size and magnitude of Christmas.
- *The Easter Story*: 1 CD; powerful Scripture passages from the Bible. Hear Max McLean recount these Scriptures that describe the most important week in human history.

CLASSIC CHRISTIAN LITERATURE AND SERMONS

- *Classics of the Christian Faith*: 9-CD set; collection of five classics: John Bunyan's *Pilgrim's Progress*; Jonathan Edwards' *Sinners in the Hands of an Angry God*; Martin Luther's *Here I Stand*; St. Augustine's *The Conversion of St. Augustine*; and George Whitefield's *The Method of Grace*.
- *Pilgrim's Progress*, by John Bunyan (1678); 5-CD set; "As I slept I dreamed a dream" — so begins Bunyan's beautiful and moving allegory of Christian, the Pilgrim, on his perilous journey to the Celestial City.
- *Sinners in the Hands of an Angry God*, by Jonathan Edwards (1741); 1 CD; the most famous and terrifying sermon ever preached on American soil by America's most revered theologian.
- *Here I Stand*, by Martin Luther (1521); 1 CD; Luther was called to defend his writings against the established church. The explosive speech he delivered decisively altered the spiritual map of the Christian world.
- *The Conversion of St. Augustine*, by St. Augustine (AD 397); 1 CD; after the conversion of St. Paul on the road to Damascus, the dramatic conversion of St. Augustine is the most significant conversion story in Christian history.
- *The Method of Grace*, by George Whitefield (c. 1760); 1 CD; Whitefield is considered one of the greatest evangelists of all

time, whose fervent message helped transform America during The Great Awakening.

- *The Valley of Vision*: 7-CD set, 6 hours; a collection of prayers and devotions taken from the writings of spiritual giants like John Bunyan, Charles Spurgeon, Isaac Watts, and Richard Baxter.

- *We Hold These Truths to Be Self-Evident*: 1 CD; four master-pieces that define our nation: The Declaration of Independence (1776), The Preamble to the Constitution (1787), The Gettysburg Address (1863), and Lincoln's Second Inaugural Address (1865).

- *A Practical View of Real Christianity*, by Willian Wilberforce (1759–1833), 1 CD. This great British statesman is best known as the driving forsce in Parliament that ended the slave trade in England. His book shows us the passion that fueled his life.

Discussion Questions for Accompanying DVD

INSTRUCTIONS: Each boldfaced header below refers to a section on the main menu of the DVD accompanying this book. The sections can be viewed in any order. Each section begins with general time estimates for usage by a class or small group. Discussion time will vary by size of class and amount of conversation for each point.

Readings That Unleash the Word

(Classes can adjust the following to take between 20 and 45 minutes)

1. Watch the opening one-minute introduction by Max McLean. This will bring you to a menu of readings: Genesis 2:18–24; Genesis 3:1–7; Psalm 23:1–6; John 20:1–18; Romans 8:28–39.
2. Pick one of the passages and practice reading it aloud before watching the corresponding video segment. Consider having two or three different readers for that same passage. What part did you find hardest? Now watch the DVD segment for that passage. How did you feel the reader handled it?
3. In what ways do you agree or disagree with Max McLean's commentary on this particular reading?
4. Repeat with other readings: practice it, discuss it, view the corresponding DVD segment, and discuss further.
5. If appropriate: talk about how your Scripture reading group could do more peer coaching with each other, offering encouragement and constructive suggestions to improve overall reading skills or to rehearse upcoming readings.

Finding the Right People

(Classes can adjust the following to take between 20 and 45 minutes)

Watch the 15-minute segment, pausing at different places for discussion as noted.

1. Begin playing the DVD. In the opening moment Max comments that 90 percent of the success of the Scripture reading program will be determined by the people you select as readers. After those words, pause the DVD to discuss how much you agree with this idea.
2. Continue playing the DVD for about four minutes. Pause after Max McLean says, "If you were asked to put together a Scripture reading program in your church, how would you start?" How would you reply? Which of the comments on the video thus far do you relate to most? Why?
3. Continue playing the DVD. Pause after Max talks about our expectation that pastors and musicians should both prepare and then asks, "Does the same thing apply for the public reading of Scripture?" What do you think?
4. Continue playing the DVD to the end of the segment. After recapping the idea of the "90 percent factor," Max expresses confidence that there are churches all over the country that can find the right people to better raise the bar for the reading of God's Word. What is the next step for raising the bar at your own church? Perhaps discuss the specific people you would like to invite, add to, or nominate to join your Scripture reading team.

PREPARING TO READ SCRIPTURE
(Classes can adjust the following to take between 10 and 45 minutes)

1. Before you watch the segment, practice reading aloud Romans 3:21–31. If possible, have everyone read the first two verses aloud. What is the hardest challenge of these two verses for you?
2. Watch the entire seven-minute clip, taking notes on how Max McLean says he prepares a reading.
3. What surprised or impressed you most about his commentary on how he prepares?
4. What elements of preparation, if any, do you think he overlooked? Why?
5. If time permits, read and discuss either (or both) of the two book segments he references: the Quick Start Reading Guide to Reading the Bible Aloud (chapter 8) or Appendix B on how Max prepares his readings.

ADDITIONAL READINGS AND DRAMATIC PRESENTATIONS BY MAX MCLEAN

(Combine both readings and dramatic presentations. Class can adjust the following to take between 20 and 45 minutes)

1. Before you watch the segment, practice reading aloud 1 Corinthians 13:1 – 13. Now watch the corresponding DVD segment. What do you learn from watching Max McLean's reading? What thoughts or ideas did he bring out that you might have done as well?

2. Repeat with John 1:1 – 14 and Romans 3:27 – 4:8.

3. Now watch at least two of Max's memorized presentations from Mark. What impacted you most about Jesus as Max presents him? What, if anything, surprised you about the impact of memorizing and performing these longer blocks of Scripture?

4. You've seen many levels of "drama" in these readings. Which level would be most appropriate for your church? What would happen if a skilled reader pushed that comfort zone just a bit through additional energy and enthusiasm?

NOTES

WHY WE WROTE THIS BOOK

1. Phone 888-876-5661 or 973-984-3400, or see www.listenersbible.com/devotionals/todays_devotional.
2. G. Robert Jacks and Gordon D. Fee, *Getting the Word Across* (Grand Rapids: Eerdmans, 1995), 21.
3. Clayton Schmit, *Public Reading of Scripture* (Nashville, TN: Abingdon, 2002), 24.

CHAPTER ONE

1. See Mark Moring. "Devilish and Divine: The Man Who Is the Voice of God and the Incarnation of Screwtape," *Christianity Today* 53/3 (March 2009): 44–47. www.christianitytoday.com/ct/2009/march/26.44.html.
2. See, for example, Whitney Shiner, *Proclaiming the Gospel: First-Century Performance of Mark* (Harrisburg, PA: Trinity Press International, 2003).
3. Several parts of this chapter are adapted from an interview between Max McLean and Tim Challies, used by permission and posted at www.challies.com/archives/interviews/an-interview-with-max-mclean.php.

CHAPTER TWO

1. See www.revealnow.com.
2. Warren Bird, "Reading Scripture the Way Jesus Did—Aloud!" *Leadership Journal* (Winter 2008), www.christianitytoday.com/le/2008/001/20.53.html.

CHAPTER THREE

1. Phone 888-876-5661 or 973-984-3400, or see www.listenersbible.com.
2. Paul Turner and Virginia Meagher, *Guide for Lectors* (Chicago: Liturgy Training Publications, 2006), 9. See also, as examples, *2 Clement* 19.1; Tertullian, *Prescription against Heretics* 41; Eusebius, *Church History* 6.43.11.

3. See William David Shiell, *Reading Acts: The Lector and the Early Christian Audience* (Boston, MA: Brill, 2004).

Chapter Four

1. We adapted this analogy from an excellent book by Clayton Schmit, *Public Reading of Scripture* (Nashville, TN: Abingdon, 2002), 15–16.
2. Martin Connell, *Workbook for Lectors and Gospel Readers, Year B, 2006* (Chicago: Liturgy Training Publications, 2005), 2.

Chapter Five

1. This "not the bore" section is inspired by, and then extensively adapted from, Charles L. Bartow's excellent book, *Effective Speech Communication in Leading Worship* (Nashville, TN: Abingdon, 1998), 85–87.
2. J. John and Mark Stibbe (compilers), *A Box of Delights: An A-Z of the Funniest, Wisest, and Most Poignant Stories, Proverbs, Jokes, and One-Liners* (Cincinnati, OH: Monarch Books, 2002), 17.

Chapter Six

1. http://www.fpatheatre.com/pdf/Screwtape_Playbill.pdf.
2. For guidance on interpreting different types of literary genre in the Bible see titles in the bibliography, especially Gordon Fee and Douglas Stuart, *How to Read the Bible for All Its Worth* (3rd ed.; Grand Rapids: Zondervan, 2003).
3. Ronald F. Youngblood, ed., *Nelson's New Illustrated Bible Dictionary: Completely Revised and Updated Edition* (Nashville, TN: Nelson, 1995).
4. Merrill Frederick Unger and W. Murray Severance, *Unger's Concise Bible Dictionary: With Complete Pronunciation Guide to Bible Names* (Grand Rapids: Baker, 1995).
5. William O. Walker, Toni Craven, and J. Andrew Dearman, *The HarperCollins Bible Pronunciation Guide* (San Francisco: HarperCollins, 1994).
6. E. N. Hamilton, ed., *Bible Names: Pronunciations and Meanings* (Kila, MT: Kessinger Publications, 2007).
7. T. S. K. Scott-Craig, *A Guide to Pronouncing Biblical Names* (New York: Morehouse Publishing, 1982).

8. W. Murray Severance and Terry Eddinger, *That's Easy for You to Say: A Guide to Pronouncing Bible Names* (Nashville, TN: Broadman and Holman, 1997).

9. Joseph M. Staudacher, *Lector's Guide to Biblical Pronunciations* (Huntington, IN: Our Sunday Visitor, 1975).

CHAPTER SEVEN

1. This analogy comes from Sister Louis Marie, O.P. Heizler, *Basic Techniques for Voice Production* (New York: Exposition Press, 1973), 20–21.

2. Chuck Jones, *Make Your Voice Heard: An Actor's Guide to Increased Dramatic Range through Vocal Training* (New York: Back Stage Books [Random House], 2005).

3. Donna Farhi, *The Breathing Book: Vitality and Good Health through Essential Breath Work* (New York: Holt, 1996).

CHAPTER EIGHT

1. Rick Warren, *The Purpose-Driven Life* (Grand Rapids: Zondervan, 2002), 17.

CHAPTER TEN

1. David Wallechinsky, *The Book of Lists* (Edingurgh: Canongate, 1977), 469–80.

2. Christopher Goodwins, *The Bible in Limerick Verse* (New York: O Books [John Hunt Publishing], 2006), #401.

3. Ramona Demery, *Let There Be Limericks* (Springville, UT: Bonneville, 1998).

4. Ibid.

5. National Congregations Study, www.soc.duke.edu/natcong.

6. Krista Petty, *Missional Households: Externally Focused Churches Discover the Value of Families That Serve* (Dallas, TX: Leadership Network, 2009). Available only via download at leadnet.org/externallyfocusedresources.

CHAPTER ELEVEN

1. Max McLean, *The Journey of Jesus: As Told by Max McLean Narrator of "The Listener's Bible"* (Nashville, TN: Nelson, 2006).

2. Published by Regal Books in Ventura, CA (2003).

3. Leadership Network, www.leadnet.org/megachurches.

4. You might enjoy some of the stories about Bible translation by Jungle Aviation, the center of Wycliffe Bible Translators, www.jaars.org/mexico_museum.shtml.

CHAPTER TWELVE

1. Andy Crouch, *Culture Making* (Downers Grove, IL: InterVarsity Press, 2008).
2. Ibid., 66–68.
3. Robert Lewis, Wayne Cordeiro, and Warren Bird, *Culture Shift: Transforming Your Church from the Inside Out* (Hoboken, NJ: Jossey-Bass, 2005), 62.
4. Ibid., 63.

ANNOTATED BIBLIOGRAPHY

Berger, Daniel R. *Oral Interpretation of the Bible*. Eugene, OR: Wipf and Stock, 2003 (144 pages). Focuses on how to interpret the various sections of the Bible: poetry, prophecy, narrative, etc.

Connell, Martin. *Workbook for Lectors and Gospel Readers 2006 Year B*. Chicago: Liturgy Training Publications, 2005 (277 pages). This workbook is published annually, rotating between church calendar years A, B, and C. Helpful Roman Catholic resource that follows the church calendar year with advice on what to emphasize and how to pronounce.

Jacks, G. Robert, and Gordon D. Fee. *Getting the Word Across: Speech Communication for Pastors and Lay Leaders*. Grand Rapids: Eerdmans, 1995 (243 pages). A helpful book covering all aspects of technique: phrasing, emphasis, imagery, gesture, diction, and vocal control, both for preaching and reading.

Lee, Charlotte. *Oral Reading of the Scriptures*. Boston: Houghton-Mifflin, 1974 (198 pages). Two chapters focus on the basics of oral interpretation, and the rest of the book explores the various literary styles of the Bible and how to interpret them as you read.

Lindvall, Ella. *Read-Aloud Bible Stories*. Volumes 1–4. Chicago: Moody Press, 1991–1995 (160 pages). This series of richly illustrated simple-text books are tremendous for reading the Bible to little ones and encouraging children to read for themselves.

McComiskey, Thomas Edward. *Reading Scripture in Public: A Guide for Preachers and Lay Readers*. Grand Rapids: Baker, 1991 (196 pages). A helpful and particularly detailed book on the oral interpretation techniques for reading the Bible in public, especially at church.

McLean, Max. *The Journey of Jesus: As Told by Max McLean Narrator of "The Listener's Bible."* Nashville, TN: Nelson, 2006 (128 pages). This book-with-DVD is a collection of thirty stories written for young readers, retelling the Savior's journey from birth to ascension.

Rang, Jack C. *How to Read the Bible Aloud: Oral Interpretation of Scripture*. Mahwah, NJ: Paulist Press, 1994 (144 pages). Three chapters focus on voice, rate, and diction, and then the bulk of the book looks at the various literary styles of the Bible and how to interpret them as you read. Also contains exercises.

Rodenburg, Patsy. *The Need for Words: Voice and Text*. New York: Theatre Arts Books, 1993 (284 pages). Technical and heady, but contains masterful insights from a Shakespearean expert on how to communicate when reading aloud or acting. Her best section is on breathing.

Schmit, Clayton J. *Public Reading of Scripture*. Nashville, TN: Abingdon, 2002 (116 pages). Seminary professor's training for pastors and lay readers on how to read Scripture aloud in church, focusing heavily on how to understand and approach the various literary styles present in the Bible.

Williamson, Audrey J. *Living Word: Reading the Scriptures in Public.* Kansas City, MO: Beacon Hill Press of Kansas City, 1987 (188 pages). Practical advice on reading, framed by sections on the voice of the interpreter (you), and the voices of poets, prophets, teachers, and storytellers (covering various sections of Scripture).

Scripture Index

SUBJECT INDEX

Acknowledgments

There are many people we want to thank for enthusiastically supporting this book-with-DVD and the message it represents.

We start with our wonderful and precious wives, Sharon McLean and Michelle Bird.

The book's helpful illustrations come from David Rodriguez, a gifted artist who works in a variety of media as his websites illustrate: www.drgorilla.com and www.artlovemagic.com.

The book's DVD work came from two talented artists, lead videographer Nathan Troester (www.nathantroester.com) and also Daniel Cassel who capably assisted.

I (Max) have been shaped and helped by the Scripture reading team at my church in Manhattan, Redeemer Presbyterian (www.redeemer.com). I especially want to thank Ellie Ellsworth, Matt Mundy, Catrina Ganey, Joe Bergquist, and Elizabeth Davis, who gave a day to be recorded and featured in this book's accompanying DVD. Others on the reading team over the years have included Tamara Brown, Yooli Chung, Georgina Corbo, Mark Delavan, Gai Grannon, Peter Hermann, Lori McNally, Melissa Ortiz, David Plant, Joe Ricci, Jaxon Ronin, Alban Sadar, Tom Schultz, Steve Shaffer, John Unruh, and Jay Yee.

Four men have been instrumental in opening up the Scripture to me in a deep, profound way. Tim Keller is my pastor at Redeemer Presbyterian Church in New York City. No one in my experience has articulated the power of the gospel to change hearts better than he. He is also a great model for articulating the faith to skeptics and unbelievers. He truly believes in the power of Jesus to change lives. A second influence is my former pastor, the late Paul Bubna at Long Hill Chapel in Chatham, New Jersey, who first made me fall in love with the Bible. A third influence is the wonderful teaching ministry of R. C. Sproul, who helped me to understand the Bible as a unified and consistent message of grace. Finally, I must mention Ravi Zacharias, whose passion for the gospel and his radically intelligent defense of it raised my sights and set a high bar for me at a very early age.

I also want to thank my worship pastor, Tom Jennings, for supporting and encouraging the start of the lay reader's ministry at Redeemer.

The King's College (www.tkc.edu), which has classrooms and conference rooms in Manhattan's Empire State Building, graciously loaned us their facilities for a day of video shooting. Special thanks to Marvin Olasky at King's who helped set it up.

Likewise, Trinity Baptist Church in Manhattan (www.trinityny.org) graciously loaned us their beautiful sanctuary to video shoot certain Scripture readings. Special thanks to senior pastor Keith Boyd and associate pastor James Leonard.

Thanks to two nearby churches in New Jersey: Christ Church, pastored by David Ireland (www.christchurchusa.org), and Liquid Church (www.liquidchurch.com), pastored by Tim Lucas, for supplying helpful footage for our DVD, featuring lay readers from their churches. Special thanks also go to their respective media directors, Steve Malave and Jessica Bancroft. Thanks also to Sammy Hargrave at St. Andrews United Methodist Church in Plano, Texas, for providing video footage.

Numerous people allowed us to interview them or they reviewed various portions of the document. They include Nader Abadir, Michelle Bird, Gerda Bodnar, Janet L. Dale, Ralph Essien, Gwen Garnett, Brent Hoffman, Akio Iyoda, Debbie James, Kep James, Sherry Jarrett, Leonard Kageler, Solomon Karunakaran, Marquis Laughlin, Naomi Hanson Luce, Esther Newell, Richard and Deb Petty, Stephanie Plagens, Bonnie Randle, Lisa Rehm, John and Janet Rehm, Esther Thompson, Khambye Yang, and the dozens of students at Alliance Theological Seminary, Nyack, New York, where Warren Bird has taught since 1985.

Not only did I speak to many of Warren's seminary classes, but as I report in chapter 1, I was influenced by many professors when I was a student there, especially Ravi Zacharias (also mentioned above), who graciously wrote the foreword to this book.

Finally a big thank you goes to our Zondervan team, especially to our publisher Paul Engle, who championed this project, and Ryan Pazdur and Verlyn Verbrugge, our editors.

Thanks also to Ben Geist as the primary designer of the cover for the book.

ABOUT THE AUTHORS

MAX MCLEAN is President of Fellowship for the Performing Arts, narrator of *The Listener's Bible*, and speaker on the radio program *Listen to the Bible*, which airs daily on over 700 radio affiliates worldwide. He is best known for his dramatic portrayal of the Bible and classic Christian literature, specifically *Mark's Gospel*, *Genesis*, and *The Screwtape Letters*. He has recorded the Bible in several translations and regularly presents dramatic presentations of the Bible and classic Christian literature to enthusiastic audiences in theaters, colleges, and houses of worship around the country. Max's life work is to recapture the rich oral tradition of telling the Bible's story with insight and appropriate dramatic expression. Max lives in New York City with his wife, Sharon. Contact information is available at www.maxmclean.com or 973–984–3400.

Warren Bird (PhD, Fordham University) is an ordained minister who oversees the research division at Leadership Network and is a regularly contributing faculty at Alliance Theological Seminary. A graduate of Wheaton College, Wheaton Graduate School, Alliance Theological Seminary, and Fordham University, he has served as pastor or associate pastor for fifteen years. He has coauthored nineteen books, all targeted to church leaders. Warren and his wife, Michelle, live just outside New York City. Contact information is available at www.warrenbird.com.